KEY SKILL ENGLISH

HIGHER LEVEL

Pat O'Shea

JUNIOR CYCLE

Preparation for
Final Examination

MENTOR

Published in 2018 by Mentor Books

43 Furze Road
Sandyford Industrial Estate
Dublin 18
Tel: 01 – 2952112 Fax: 01 – 2952114

Website: www.mentorbooks.ie
Email: admin@mentorbooks.ie

Edited by: Linda Richardson
Design & Layout: Kathryn O'Sullivan

ISBN: 978-1-909417-89-2

1 3 5 7 9 10 8 6 4 2
Printed in Ireland

Contents

ACKNOWLEDGEMENTS

The publishers would like to thank the following for kind permission to reproduce material:

Bloomsbury Publishing Plc. For an extract from *Alphabetical Order* by Michael Frayn; Peters Fraser & Dunlop for *Tarantella* from Complete Verse by Hilaire Belloc; Carcenet Press Ltd for *Quarantine* from New Selected Poems 2013 by Eavan Boland; Praise song for my *Mother* from The Fat Black Woman's Poems © Grace Nichols 1984. Reproduced with permission of Curtis Brown Group Ltd, London on behalf of Grace Nichols; Edwin A. Romond for permission to re-print his poem *Seeing and Believing*; Faber and Faber Ltd of *Lovers on Aran* by Seamus Heaney from *Death of a Naturalist*, 1966; The Estate of George Sassoon for *Base Details*, copyright Siegfried Sassoon, by kind permission.

DEDICATION
For Emil: 'May you *live* all the days of your life'.

(Jonathan Swift)

Final Assessment Examination

1. General Information

As part of your assessment in English for your Junior Cycle, you will be required to do a Final Assessment Examination at the end of your Third Year which will be worth 180 marks - 90% of your overall grade.

There will be one examination paper which incorporates an answer booklet. It will present you with stimulus material (previously unseen material) and will also be linked thematically to the texts you have been working with during Second and Third Year. You will have two hours to complete the paper.

This Final Assessment Examination requires you to:

● Read and engage with texts
● Comprehend what you have read
● Respond to what you have read

2. Content and Format

The content and format of the examination papers may vary from year to year, so you need to read the instructions on the front of the paper very carefully; take careful note of the marks for each question and complete the tasks within the time limit provided on the front page of the exam paper.

The front page of the exam booklet will state:

● the year and the day of the examination.
● the exact time, e.g. Morning 9:30 to 11:30.
● the level, e.g. Higher or Ordinary Level English.
● the number of marks for the entire paper
● a box for your examination number (you must write this in the box)
● a box for the Centre Stamp (that will be filled in for you)

The second page of the exam booklet:

The paper may be given a **theme** which will be clearly stated at the top of the second page of the exam paper.

You will then be given clear instructions regarding the **number of sections** and the **number of questions** which you must answer. These will change from year to year. For example, a section might be referred to as: **Section A. Reading Texts to Understand - Shakespearean Drama**. This will be followed by the number of marks for the section and the number of questions which you must answer.

Each section will be worth a stated number of marks which will be divided up depending on the questions set. You will be given an indication of how much time to spend on each section and you should make sure you don't exceed the time limits.

The questions don't carry equal marks, so you need to **pay careful attention to the space allowed in the booklet** and the **marks for each question**. The marks will be stated at the top of each question. Space to write your answers will be provided after each question. Space is also provided for extra work. Label any extra work clearly with the question number and part.

3. Answering on Studied Material

When answering on studied material you must use texts prescribed for examination in that year.

You must study a Shakespearean play for Higher Level and one other play. You also need to study two novels, a selection of short stories and a selection of poetry.

A film, biography, travel text or documentary can be chosen from the prescribed list of texts.

Clearly state the title of your studied texts and the name of the author when answering questions.

In addition to the studied texts, you will need to be familiar with and have practice with reading and writing in a variety of styles and for different audiences and purposes.

4. Grading of the Final Examination

Distinction =	>90 to 100 marks.
Higher Merit =	>75 and < 90 marks.
Merit =	>55 and <75.
Achieved =	>40 and <55.
Partially Achieved =	>20 and <40.
(not graded) =	> 0 and < 20.

5. Tips to Aid Exam Success

If there is any background information given for a text or extract, read it very carefully as it will contain essential information to help you understand the context of the passage.

Note how many marks are being awarded for each question. The length of your answer will be related to the question and the time at your disposal. The space allowed in the answer book after each question will also give you an idea of how much you should write. Just make sure that you do not exceed the time indicated for each section.

Make sure that you include a personal approach in your answers where possible. For example:

> 'I think this because . . .'

> 'In my opinion . . .'

> 'Personally, I dislike this character because . . .'

Such personal comments are essential when you are asked for your impression or your opinion in the question.

This book has been written to help you to practise and revise the Key Skills required in order to do well in the Final Assessment Examination.

Note: For purposes of clarity, the chapters in this book have been divided into Drama, Fiction, Poetry, Literacy and the Mechanics of Language. These sections will overlap with a wide variety of written material and will encourage you to respond creatively, using all the skills you have acquired over the last three years.

01 Drama

This unit addresses the following learning outcomes:
OL8, R1, 2, 3, 4, 6, 7, 8, 9; W1, 3, 7, 8, 9.

Introduction

As part of your Final Assessment Examination, you may be required to answer questions on **unseen drama** and **studied drama**. The specification requires Higher Level students to study the full text of a prescribed Shakespearean play. It is essential that you have a clear understanding of all aspects of dramatic structure and techniques and that you are familiar with critical terms used when discussing plays. You may also need to be able to link an unseen extract with the play which you have studied in class.

Key Skills for Answering on Drama:
When you write about drama you must display an ability to understand and interpret what you read. In your response you are expected to make relevant points, which you can support with reference to the text. You need to understand each of the following key areas:
● Setting ● Stagecraft ● Character
● Mood or Atmosphere ● Plot

A. Key Skills for Understanding Shakespearean Drama

William Shakespeare (1564-1616) is considered to be the greatest playwright and poet in English literature. His plays are generally categorised as (a) **Tragedies,** (b) **Comedies** and (c) **Histories**. For Junior Cycle Higher Level English, you must study a Shakespearean play. The Final Assessment (i.e. written exam at the end of Third Year) will probably examine your ability to engage meaningfully with the text and test your understanding of how the plays are crafted and constructed.

(a) **Tragedies** by Shakespeare may involve some funny moments, but tend towards more **serious, dramatic plots and themes** with endings that involve the deaths of the main characters. In these plays there is a sense that events are inevitable or inescapable and that human beings are, by nature, flawed or imperfect. Examples of famous Shakespearean tragedies are *Romeo and Juliet, King Lear, Hamlet* and *Macbeth.*

(b) **Comedies** by Shakespeare are not what modern audiences would necessarily find funny. In spite of some very dramatic storylines, such as in *The Merchant of Venice,* usually what defines a Shakespearean play as a comedy is that it has **a happy ending**, often involving celebration and marriage. *As You Like It, The Taming of the Shrew, Much Ado About Nothing, A Midsummer Night's Dream* and *The Comedy of Errors* are well-known comedies.

(c) **Histories** by Shakespeare focus on English monarchs. They usually play upon Elizabethan propaganda, showing the dangers of civil war and glorifying the queen's Tudor ancestors. *King John, Richard II, Richard III, Henry IV, Henry V, Henry VI* and *Henry VIII* fall into this category of history play.

1. The Structure of Shakespeare's Plays

Shakespeare's plays have **a five-act structure.** Each act is divided into **scenes.** Although the number of scenes in each act may change, the five-act structure does not change.

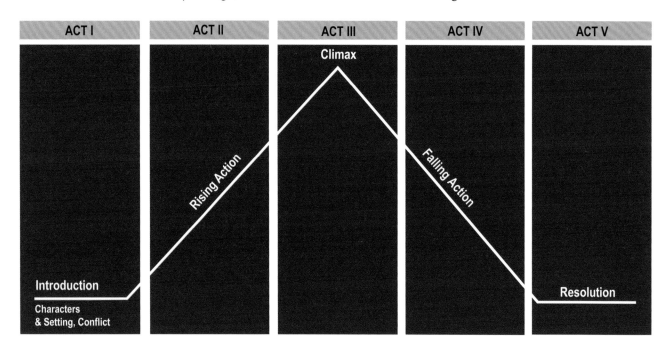

Act I: Introduction

In this act, the major themes and the main **characters** of the play are introduced. The **setting** is established and some major **conflict** is identified.

Act II: Rising Action

During the Rising Action, the basic conflict introduced in Act I is made **more complicated** by other conflicts and obstacles facing the main character or characters. For this reason, the Rising Action is sometimes called the **Complication.**

Act III: Climax

The climax of a play is also known as the **turning point**. The climax marks **a notable change,** for better or worse, in the plot. This point begins in Act III and builds up in a series of events. This is where **most of the drama or action** takes place.

Act IV: Falling Action

During the Falling Action, the conflict reaches a high point and a clear winner and loser are determined. This act may also contain a final moment of **suspense,** in which the outcome might be uncertain.

Act V: Resolution

The **Resolution** brings all loose ends together and concludes the story. All of the **conflicts are resolved** and life returns to a new normal – even though things have changed. In traditional comedies, the ending leaves the main character/s better off than at the start, while traditional tragedies end in catastrophe and death.

2. Use of Verse

Modern plays are usually written in prose, although some songs or verse could occur incidentally in the course of the plot. If you quickly flick through a copy of a Shakespeare play, you will see at a glance that the text looks quite different on the page. It is mainly a type of verse with some occasional use of prose.

Verse is easily recognisable because it appears in narrow blocks. On the left-hand side of the page, the lines all begin with capital letters and are aligned; however, the ends of the lines create a jagged, unequal appearance. There are two main types of verse – rhymed and blank.

(a) Rhymed verse

Rhymed verse usually takes the form of **rhyming couplets,** i.e. two successive lines of verse where **the final words rhyme**. These rhymes are very easy to hear when you read the text aloud. If you give a letter to each rhyme, the pattern would be aa bb cc etc.

Look at this example from *A Midsummer Night's Dream:*

Love looks not with the eyes, but with the **mind**;	a
And therefore is winged Cupid painted **blind**.	a
Nor hath Love's mind of any judgement **taste**;	b
Wings, and no eyes, figure unheedy **haste**:	b
And therefore is Love said to be a **child**,	c
Because in choice he is so oft **beguiled**.	c

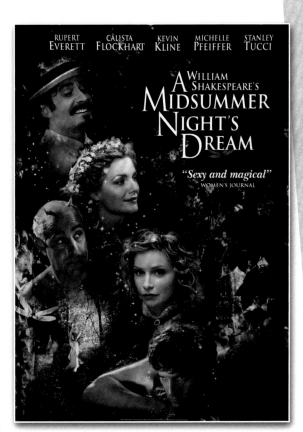

RUPERT EVERETT · CALISTA FLOCKHART · KEVIN KLINE · MICHELLE PFEIFFER · STANLEY TUCCI

A WILLIAM SHAKESPEARE'S MIDSUMMER NIGHT'S DREAM

"Sexy and magical"
WOMEN'S JOURNAL

Notice how the capital letters at the start of each line are arranged in a neat column on the left-hand side, while the right-hand side is uneven and appears to slope inwards, although this will not always be the case. The important thing is that **each pair of lines (couplets) rhyme**.

Rhymed verse can also use other rhyming patterns. For example, in this extract from *Much Ado About Nothing* **alternate lines rhyme**.

Good morrow, masters; put your torches **out**:	a
The wolves have prey'd; and look, the gentle **day**,	b
Before the wheels of Phoebus, round **about**	a
Dapples the drowsy east with spots of **grey**.	b

Rhyme is used for lyrical passages and for songs. It is also used to give advice or point out a moral. Sometimes, rhyme is used for comic effect (for example, the Pyramus and Thisbe play in *A Midsummer Night's Dream).*

A single rhymed couplet may also appear at the end of a speech. It has the effect of adding a sense of **completion or finality** to the speech:

> I'll so offend to make offence a **skill**
> Redeeming time when men think least I **will**.
> (*Henry IV*, 1.2)

(b) Blank verse

Blank verse is different to rhymed verse because although each line begins with a capital letter, **the lines do not rhyme**. Look carefully at this extract from *Henry IV, Part 1* taking note of the capital letter at the beginning of each line and the lack of end-line rhyme:

> KING HENRY IV
> But I have sent for him to answer this;
> And for this cause awhile we must neglect
> Our holy purpose to Jerusalem.
> Cousin, on Wednesday next our council we
> Will hold at Windsor; so inform the lords:
> But come yourself with speed to us again;
> For more is to be said and to be done
> Than out of anger can be uttered.

(c) Rhythm in Shakespearean verse

Rhythm is also very important in Shakespearean verse. Each line usually has 10 syllables which are arranged in a pattern of unstressed and stressed syllables. This pattern is known as **iambic pentameter.** An **iamb** is a measurement of two syllables where the first is unstressed and the second is stressed. **Pentameter** means that there are five (from the Greek word 'penta' = 5) stresses per line.

A good example of this can be seen in Romeo's famous line from *Romeo and Juliet* when he sees Juliet appear at her window. We call beating out the rhythm of a line like this **scansion.** We **scan** the lines for the rhythm.

> But SOFT, /what LIGHT / through YON/der WIN/dow BREAKS.

If you say that line aloud, you can hear a rhythmic pattern:
da-DUM, da-DUM, da-DUM, da-DUM, da-DUM.

Another example can be seen in Portia's speech from *The Merchant of Venice* – watch out for the word 'quality' which has three syllables!

> The QUAL/ i TY/ of MER/cy IS/ not STRAINED

Although most of Shakespeare's plays are written in blank verse with a rhythm of iambic pentameter, the rhythm can vary. Some lines may have an extra syllable in a line or some may have less than 10 syllables.

Blank verse is used throughout Shakespeare's plays in a wide range of situations because it comes close to natural speaking rhythms. It is used mainly for passionate, lofty or special occasions and may suggest the refinement of a character.

Many **monologues** and **soliloquies** are written in blank verse.
A **monologue** is a speech where a character speaks alone but is addressing other characters. An example of this could be a king addressing his troops before a battle.

A **soliloquy** is a speech meant to be heard only by the audience. It reveals a character's private thoughts. The character is usually alone on the stage during a soliloquy.

'But soft, what light through yonder window breaks'
Romeo and Juliet

(d) Prose in Shakespeare's plays

Prose is like ordinary speech with no regular pattern of rhythm. It interrupts the rhythmic pattern of blank verse.
It is very easy to recognise prose because it is printed in the text just like an ordinary paragraph from a novel or short story. If you are not certain whether a passage is in prose or in blank verse, look for the following clue: **if every new line begins with a capital letter, it is verse; if not, it is prose.**

Look at the following use of prose in an extract from *A Midsummer Night's Dream*:

QUINCE
Is all our company here?

BOTTOM
You were best to call them generally, man by man, according to the scrip.

QUINCE
Here is the scroll of every man's name, which is thought fit, through all Athens, to play in our interlude before the duke and the duchess, on his wedding-day at night.

Notice that the lines **do not begin with capital letters** and there is **no use of rhyme**. Therefore, it is **prose.**

Shakespeare uses prose for several reasons. It is often used to indicate characters who are mad or going mad (as in *King Lear*); to distinguish lower-class characters from their superiors; to poke fun at characters who are behaving in a ridiculous manner (the Mechanicals in *A Midsummer Night's Dream)*; and to allow for short, functional lines like 'And I, my lord,' and 'I pray you leave me' in order to give the play a sense of realism. Prose is also used for letters which characters write to others (as in *Macbeth*).

Much Ado About Nothing is one of the few plays by Shakespeare where the majority of the text is written in prose. Substantial verse sections, nevertheless, are used to achieve a lofty, dignified tone or to express emotion and energy.

3. Engaging with and Responding to a Shakespearean Drama Extract

If the stimulus material (**unseen material**) on your exam paper is taken from a play, you may be given a short introduction to the extract so that you understand the **background** of the scene.

You will need to know the setting, who the characters are, the relationships between the characters and what has happened so far in the plot. This information provides you with **context** (background) for the extract. Read all background information very carefully as you may be questioned about it.

Pages 15–22 contain examples of (a) background information and questions and (b) short extracts and questions. The plays are: **1.** *As You Like It*, **2.** *All's Well That Ends Well* and **3.** *The Taming of the Shrew*.

1 *As You Like It*

(a) Background information and questions

In the comedy *As You Like It*, Celia and her cousin Rosalind are as close as sisters. Rosalind is the daughter of Duke Senior, whose throne has been usurped (taken by force) by his brother, Frederick. Frederick, Celia's father, has banished Duke Senior, along with a band of his faithful followers, to the Forest of Arden to live the life of simple foresters. Until now, it is only the strong bond between Rosalind and Celia that prevents Duke Frederick from sending Rosalind away to share her father's exile. In the extract which follows, Frederick storms into the palace, accuses Rosalind of plotting against him, and, despite Celia's pleas for her cousin, banishes Rosalind.

A production of *As You Like It* showing Celia and Rosalind, staged at Shakespeare's Globe Theatre.

The following questions on the background information should be answered as briefly as possible.

1. How are Celia and Rosalind related to each other? _____

2. How are Frederick and Rosalind related to each other? _____

3. Who has usurped the throne of Duke Senior? _____

4. Where is Rosalind when she hears about her banishment? _____

5. What two settings are mentioned? _____

(b) Extract and questions

SCENE I *The Forest of Arden*

Enter DUKE SENIOR, AMIENS, *and two or three Lords, like foresters*

DUKE SENIOR
Now, my co-mates and brothers in exile,
Hath not old custom made this life more sweet
Than that of painted pomp? Are not these woods
More free from peril than the envious court?
Here feel we but the penalty of Adam,
The seasons' difference, as the icy fang   .
And churlish* chiding of the winter's wind,
Which, when it bites and blows upon my body,
Even till I shrink with cold, I smile and say
'This is no flattery: these are counsellors
That feelingly persuade me what I am.'
Sweet are the uses of adversity,
Which, like the toad, ugly and venomous,
Wears yet a precious jewel in his head;
And this our life exempt from public haunt
Finds tongues in trees, books in the running brooks,
Sermons in stones and good in every thing.
I would not change it.

AMIENS
Happy is your grace,
That can translate the stubbornness of fortune
Into so quiet and so sweet a style.

DUKE SENIOR
Come, shall we go and kill us venison?
And yet it irks me the poor dappled fools,
Being native burghers* of this desert city,
Should in their own confines with forked heads
Have their round haunches gored.

churlish = rude, ill-mannered
burghers= citizens

Questions

In each case, write the letter corresponding to the correct answer in the appropriate box.

1. What is Duke Senior's attitude to being banished to the Forest of Arden? ☐

    A. He is resentful of his brother's actions and wishes to get revenge.

    B. He feels safer in the forest than he did in the court.

    C. He finds it difficult to endure the harsh winter conditions.

2. Which of the following is the best interpretation of the lines: ☐

    And this our life exempt from public haunt

    Finds tongues in trees, books in the running brooks,

    Sermons in stones and good in every thing.

    A. We are better off being close to nature, where we can learn about life, than being among crowds of people.

    B. We are denied the company of others and must be content with what nature has to offer.

    C. We will have to use our imaginations to survive in the forest.

3. What does the Duke mean when he says: ☐

    Sweet are the uses of adversity,

    Which, like the toad, ugly and venomous,

    Wears yet a precious jewel in his head;

    A. You have to make the best of a bad situation.

    B. There is no point in complaining about hardship.

    C. There are positive aspects to even the ugliest of misfortunes.

4. Which of the following statements about the extract is true? ☐

    A. It is written in prose

    B. It uses rhyming couplets

    C. It uses blank verse

2 *All's Well That Ends Well*

(a) Background information and questions

The central action of *All's Well That Ends Well* concerns Helena, a beautiful woman, and her pursuit of a man of higher social position than herself in the French court of Rousillon. Helena is the daughter of a court physician who has recently died. The man whom she pursues is Bertram, a young man of the nobility, who is in mourning for his dead father, the Count.

1. Where is this play set? _____
2. What do Helena and Bertram have in common?_____
3. Whose father was once a doctor? _____
4. Who is being pursued in this play? _____
5. Why do you think Helena may be considered unsuitable to marry Bertram? _____

(b) Extract and questions

In the following scene, after Bertram departs from the court to live in Paris, Helena delivers a soliloquy.

HELENA

O, were that all! I think not on my father;
And these great tears grace his remembrance more
Than those I shed for him. What was he like?
I have forgot him: my imagination
Carries no favour in't but Bertram's.
I am undone: there is no living, none,
If Bertram be away. 'Twere all one
That I should love a bright particular star
And think to wed it, he is so above me:
In his bright radiance and collateral light
Must I be comforted, not in his sphere.
The ambition in my love thus plagues itself:
The hind* that would be mated by the lion
Must die for love. 'Twas pretty, though plague,
To see him every hour; to sit and draw
His arched brows, his hawking* eye, his curls,
In our heart's table; heart too capable
Of every line and trick* of his sweet favour:
But now he's gone, and my idolatrous fancy
Must sanctify his relics*. Who comes here?

hind = deer
hawking = hawk-like, sharp
trick = distinguishing feature
relics = what remains (in this case, the memory of him)

In each case write the letter corresponding to the correct answer in the appropriate box.

1. Why is Helena so distressed in this soliloquy? ☐
    A. She is mourning her father's death.
    B. She is lamenting the loss of Bertram.
    C. She is grieving for the loss of both her father and Bertram.

2. What does Helena mean when she says,
   'Twas pretty, though plague,
   To see him every hour
   A. I enjoyed his company every day.
   B. Even though there was a plague, we spent hours together.
   C. It was delightful, but also tormenting, to be in his presence so often.

3. Which of the following best describes this soliloquy?
   A. It is written in prose
   B. It is written in blank verse.
   C. It is written in rhyming couplets.

3   *The Taming of the Shrew*

(a) Background information and questions

The scene which follows is taken from Shakespeare's play *The Taming of the Shrew*. Lucentio, a Florentine traveller, has come to study in Padua in Italy and is accompanied by his servant Tranio. Upon their arrival, they see Baptista Minola, a rich gentleman of Padua, approaching with his two daughters, Katherine and her younger sister Bianca, as well as Gremio and Hortensio, both suitors to Bianca (they wish to marry her). Baptista is in the process of rejecting both suitors for Bianca because Katherine, who is a sharp-tongued girl, must get married before he will allow her younger sister to do so.

Questions
?

1. Where is this play set?
2. What is the relationship between Tranio and Lucentio?
3. What is the relationship between Gremio and Bianca?
4. Why does Baptista Minola reject the suitors of Bianca?
5. Why do you think Katherine doesn't have a suitor?

Unit 1: Drama

(b) Extract and questions

BAPTISTA

Gentlemen, importune* me no farther,
For how I firmly am resolved you know;
That is, not bestow my youngest daughter
Before I have a husband for the elder:
If either of you both love Katherine,
Because I know you well and love you well,
Leave shall you have to court her at your pleasure.

GREMIO

[*Aside*] To cart her rather: she's too rough for me.
There, there, Hortensio, will you any wife?

KATHERINE

I pray you, sir, is it your will
To make a stale of me amongst these mates?

HORTENSIO

Mates, maid! how mean you that? no mates for you,
Unless you were of gentler, milder mould.

KATHERINE

I'faith, sir, you shall never need to fear:
Iwis* it is not half way to her heart;
But if it were, doubt not her care should be
To comb your noddle with a three-legg'd stool
And paint your face and use you like a fool.

HORTENSIO

From all such devils, good Lord deliver us!

GREMIO

And me too, good Lord!

TRANIO

Hush, master! here's some good pastime toward:
That wench is stark mad or wonderful froward*.

LUCENTIO

But in the other's silence do I see
Maid's mild behaviour and sobriety*.

Katherine is a sharp-tongued girl who is unwilling to be married off to one of her younger sister's suitors.

importune = annoy with persistent requests
iwis = certainly
froward = forward, saucy
sobriety = calmness, dignity

Questions

1. Identify a rhyming couplet in the extract on page 21 and comment on its function.

2. Write the letter corresponding to the correct answer in the appropriate box.

   Why does Baptista want Katherine to marry before Bianca? ☐

   A. Because she is the elder daughter and should marry first.
   B. Because he is more attached to Bianca and wants to keep her at home.
   C. Because he knows Katherine is a problem and is trying to get her a husband by using a form of blackmail.

3. Which one of these statements is true? ☐

   A. The first four lines of this extract are written in iambic pentameter.
   B. Part of this extract is written in prose.
   C. There is no use of either iambic pentameter or prose.

B. Key Skills for Analysing a Shakespearean Scene

Always remember that plays are written to be performed on stage. When you are responding to questions on drama, imagine that you are a member of the audience. Do not write about a scene in the same way as you would about an extract from fiction. Show awareness of the fact that it is written to be performed on stage before an audience. You need to understand each of the following key areas:

1. Setting
2. Mood or Atmosphere
3. Stagecraft
4. Character
5. Plot

1. Setting

The setting of a play refers to the **location** and the **time of the action**.

The setting of a scene is not always of great importance. However, if the playwright has provided details about the setting, you must look for a reason for this. The setting can create a certain atmosphere or give an indication of the time, place, period in history or any other information that can influence how you interpret events and characters. For example, a daughter arguing with her father in a modern setting is a very different situation to a daughter arguing with her father during earlier centuries, when daughters were expected to obey their fathers without question. Likewise, the theft of a small item that takes place against a background of wealth and luxury may be interpreted differently from a similar theft in a setting which depicts poverty and deprivation.

If the setting influences the plot, the characters, the atmosphere or any other aspect of the play or extract, you must be able to discuss it and demonstrate its importance.

Reading texts to understand how setting is created:

The following is the opening scene from Shakespeare's tragedy *Hamlet*.

Background information

Three soldiers, Francisco, Bernardo and Marcellus are on night guard in the castle of Elsinore in Denmark. The ghost of a dead king has appeared to them twice and they have decided to ask a man, called Horatio, to witness the next appearance of the ghost. Horatio does not believe in ghosts.

᪤ ACT I ᪣

SCENE I. Elsinore. A platform before the castle.

FRANCISCO at his post. Enter BERNARDO

BERNARDO
Who's there?

FRANCISCO
Nay, answer me: stand, and unfold* yourself.

BERNARDO
Long live the king!

FRANCISCO
Bernardo?

BERNARDO
He.

FRANCISCO
You come most carefully* upon your hour.

BERNARDO
'Tis now struck twelve; get thee to bed, Francisco.

FRANCISCO

For this relief much thanks: 'tis bitter cold,
And I am sick at heart.

BERNARDO

Have you had quiet guard?

FRANCISCO

Not a mouse stirring.

BERNARDO

Well, good night.
If you do meet Horatio and Marcellus,
The rivals* of my watch, bid them make haste.

FRANCISCO

I think I hear them. Stand, ho! Who's there?

Enter HORATIO and MARCELLUS

HORATIO

Friends to this ground.

MARCELLUS

And liegemen* to the Dane*.

FRANCISCO

Give you good night.

MARCELLUS

O, farewell, honest soldier:
Who hath relieved you?

FRANCISCO

Bernardo has my place.
Give you good night.

Exit

MARCELLUS

Holla! Bernardo!

BERNARDO

Say,
What, is Horatio there?

HORATIO

A piece of him.

BERNARDO

Welcome, Horatio: welcome, good Marcellus.

MARCELLUS

What, has this thing appear'd again to-night?

BERNARDO

I have seen nothing.

MARCELLUS

Horatio says 'tis but our fantasy,
And will not let belief take hold of him
Touching this dreaded sight, twice seen of us:
Therefore I have entreated him along
With us to watch the minutes of this night;
That if again this apparition come,
He may approve our eyes and speak to it.

HORATIO

Tush, tush, 'twill not appear.

unfold = declare who you are

carefully = punctually

rivals = companions

liegemen = loyal subjects

Dane = King of Denmark

Questions

Engaging and responding

1. How do you know that this scene is set at night? Give at least two reasons.

2. Would it make any difference if it were set during daylight hours? Explain.

3. What does Francisco **say** and **do** which shows he is very frightened?

4. Why do you think Bernardo wants Horatio and Marcellus to 'make haste'?

5. How does the setting contribute to the fear experienced by the soldiers?

6. Why do you think the lines are so short for most of this opening scene?

7. How does the attitude of Horatio contrast with that of the other soldiers?

8. Bearing in mind your answers to questions 1-7, explain how tension or suspense is created in this extract with special mention of the part played by setting. Support your points with quotation from the extract.

9. Which of the following images, in your opinion, most successfully captures the atmosphere and setting of this extract? Explain your choice.

10. **Making Connections:** Name a Shakespearean play which you have studied during Junior Cycle. Describe the setting in any scene of this play and write three paragraphs about (a) the importance of the setting to the plot, (b) the way atmosphere is created in this scene and (c) how the setting influenced the way you reacted to the characters.

More about Setting in Shakespearean Plays

It is important to remember that Shakespeare used very few props (objects) or scenery, which meant that the audience had to use their imaginations. The extract from the opening of Hamlet would have been performed in broad daylight although it takes place at night. The audience at that time would have to imagine the setting and the time of the action. They depended completely on what the characters **said** and **did** in order to get a sense of where the action was taking place and what time of day or night it was. Also, it is important to remember how we experience a play in the theatre – we can't pause the action or fast-forward, like we can when watching a film on television! Neither can we rewind or ask the actors to repeat their lines. For instance, in the scene from *Hamlet*, we have to think about how the audience would have experienced it and how closely they would need to listen to the spoken word to make sense of the action. So word-choice was a very important part of the playwright's skill.

If we were producing a play by Shakespeare for a modern audience, we would have more choices. We could try to create the locations with a naturalistic set, but this would create a lot of problems as all of Shakespeare's plays have several locations and they change very abruptly. We could use some abstract or symbolic props and allow them to suggest the setting or, like Shakespeare, we could use an empty space and allow the words spoken by the characters, the 'word scenery', to create the setting.

Tip:

For your studied Shakespearean play, in addition to the general setting, you will also need to be aware of where specific scenes are set and when locations change. Remember, you are dealing with the entire play, as opposed to a short extract such as those given in unseen drama.

2. Mood or Atmosphere

The mood or atmosphere in a scene creates a big impact on the audience. Ask yourself questions about the mood of the play.

(a) What is the mood at the beginning of the extract?

(b) How is this mood created?

(c) Does the mood change in the course of the extract?

(d) How does it change?

(e) Why does it change?

(f) Is the audience aware of something that the characters are not aware of?

> **Tip:**
> For your studied play you will need to go into greater depth. For each of the above areas for discussion, ensure that you can quote accurately and/ or use close textual reference to support your points.

Because you will be dealing with an entire play, as opposed to a short extract, you will need to be aware of the changing moods in different scenes of your chosen play.

Be prepared to select **specific scenes** to illustrate **how the playwright creates mood or atmosphere**. Be able to pinpoint scenes where the mood changes gradually or abruptly and show how this is achieved. Characterisation, dialogue, actions and consequences of actions will all affect the mood of the play.

Read this next extract from Shakespeare's tragedy *Macbeth*, paying very close attention to the language used to create the setting and mood.

Background information

In this extract, Macbeth and his fellow soldier, Banquo, are returning home after winning a ferocious battle against the enemies of their king. They are happy to have won the battle but find the stormy weather quite alarming. Unknown to Banquo, Macbeth has secret hopes of one day becoming King of Scotland himself. On their way, they meet three witches who seem to know what the future holds.

MACBETH

So foul and fair a day I have not seen.

BANQUO

How far is't call'd to Forres? What are these
So wither'd and so wild in their attire,
That look not like the inhabitants o' the earth,
And yet are on't? Live you? or are you aught*
That man may question? You seem to understand me,
By each at once her chappy finger laying
Upon her skinny lips: you should be women,
And yet your beards forbid me to interpret
That you are so.

MACBETH

Speak, if you can: what are you?

FIRST WITCH

All hail, Macbeth! hail to thee, thane* of Glamis!

SECOND WITCH

All hail, Macbeth, hail to thee, thane of Cawdor!

THIRD WITCH

All hail, Macbeth, thou shalt be king hereafter!

BANQUO

Good sir, why do you start; and seem to fear
Things that do sound so fair? I' the name of truth,
Are ye fantastical, or that indeed
Which outwardly ye show? My noble partner
You greet with present grace and great prediction
Of noble having and of royal hope,
That he seems rapt withal: to me you speak not.
If you can look into the seeds of time,
And say which grain will grow and which will not,
Speak then to me, who neither beg nor fear
Your favours nor your hate.

FIRST WITCH
Hail!

SECOND WITCH
Hail!

THIRD WITCH
Hail!

FIRST WITCH
Lesser than Macbeth, and greater.

SECOND WITCH
Not so happy, yet much happier.

THIRD WITCH
Thou shalt get* kings, though thou be none:
So all hail, Macbeth and Banquo!

FIRST WITCH
Banquo and Macbeth, all hail!

MACBETH
Stay, you imperfect speakers, tell me more:
By Sinel's* death I know I am thane of Glamis;
But how of Cawdor? the thane of Cawdor lives,
A prosperous gentleman; and to be king
Stands not within the prospect of belief,
No more than to be Cawdor. Say from whence
You owe this strange intelligence? or why
Upon this blasted heath you stop our way
With such prophetic greeting? Speak, I charge you.

Witches vanish

BANQUO
The earth hath bubbles, as the water has,
And these are of them. Whither* are they vanish'd?

MACBETH
Into the air; and what seem'd corporal melted
As breath into the wind. Would* they had stay'd!

aught = anything
thane = a Scottish earl
get = be the father of
Sinel = the father of Macbeth
whither = where
would = I wish

Engaging and responding

1. What evidence, **from the words spoken by the characters**, suggest that this scene takes place outdoors and in bad weather?

2. What sort of atmosphere is created by the numerous questions in this extract? Explain your answer.

3. How does the appearance and disappearance of the witches influence the atmosphere of this extract?

4. In what way is Banquo's reaction to the witches different from that of Macbeth? Explain.

5. The witches' answers are full of contradictions. Identify three contradictory phrases and say what effect these have on the general atmosphere.

6. Banquo says: 'you should be women, / And yet your beards forbid me to interpret / That you are so'. Rewrite these lines in your own words.

7. Taking into consideration your answers to questions 1-6 above, write a paragraph describing the setting and atmosphere created in this extract.

8. If you were directing this scene, how would you like Macbeth's speech to the witches to be performed? Refer to tone of voice, body language and facial expression.

9. Imagine that you are Macbeth. Write a diary entry based on this experience.

10. You are another soldier and have heard rumours about this incident. Write a letter to Banquo telling him what you have heard and questioning him about what happened.

3. Stagecraft

Stagecraft is not the same thing as setting or stage directions, although these may contribute. When you write about how you would stage an extract or scene, you are writing about **the play in performance** on stage.

You could refer to such things as props, costume, lighting, sound, backdrops or any other technique which you think would bring the play alive for a modern audience and create a vivid, realistic impact.

Tip:
From a Shakespearean play which you have studied, it is advisable to select at least three key scenes – the opening, climax and closing scenes are particularly important – and be able to write a reasonably detailed analysis of how they could be performed successfully.

If you are asked to comment on **how you would direct the scene**, you would need to include **stage directions, instructions to actors regarding facial expressions, gestures, movements, tone of voice,** etc. In other words, **imagine** the scene in your head and **describe** it in as much detail as you can. Be sure to **explain why you would use certain techniques** and the impact you would be attempting to achieve.

It is a good idea to prepare **a short list of props** for each of three key scenes in the play and also a short list of **appropriate lighting, sound effects and costumes**. Be ready to explain why you have chosen each item on these lists.

Making connections: From a Shakespearean play which you have studied, select a scene which has a very dramatic setting. How would you produce this scene on a modern stage in order to highlight the location, atmosphere and the interaction of the characters?

Tip:
Never forget that plays are written to be performed on stage. When you are responding to questions show awareness of the fact that the play is written to be performed on stage before an audience.

Sample Question and Answer on Setting

Name a Shakespearean play which you have studied during Junior Cycle. Describe the setting in any scene of this play and write three paragraphs about (a) the importance of the setting to the plot, (b) the way atmosphere is created in this scene and (c) how the scene influenced the way you reacted to the characters.

Answer

The Shakespearean play I have studied is *Romeo and Juliet* and the scene which I have chosen is the brawl scene from the opening scene of the play.

(a) The play, as we are told by the Prologue, is set in Italy in the 'fair' city of Verona. Shakespeare does not flesh out the details, but we can deduce from the language that it is quite a large, lively and bustling city. The fact that the servants belong to two different 'houses' which bear an 'ancient grudge', suggests that the city has been long-established and that very wealthy families, who can afford large numbers of servants, have been living there for a very long time. When the brawl breaks out between feuding members of the Capulets and Montagues, citizens enter the brawl shouting 'Down with the Capulets! Down with the Montagues!'. From this detail, we see that the feud is deeply affecting the general population of the city. The fact that a Prince resides in Verona further emphasises its size and importance. The Prince gives us the information that there have already been, 'Three civil brawls, bred of an airy word', but also refers to what was once 'the quiet of our streets'. This suggests to me that Verona was once a law-abiding city where people could live in peace, but that this has now changed and the streets are dangerous places to roam. This setting is important because many significant events take place on the streets of Verona. It is here that Romeo receives the news about the Capulet ball. It is here that Tybalt kills Mercutio and in turn, is slain himself. The heat associated with an inland location in Italy also contributes to the feeling that people can get overheated and that passions can be easily aroused.

(b) The atmosphere in this scene is skilfully created by the language and imagery used by the feuding servants. Images of love and sex are mingled with images of violence and death when Sampson refers to his 'naked weapon', makes bawdy jokes about cutting off the 'maidenheads' of the Montague women and creates puns on the words 'thrust' and 'strike'. The audience of the time would have probably found the jokes and puns on words amusing, creating an atmosphere of comedy, but I personally think that the atmosphere is more threatening than funny. The threat of the Prince changes the mood: 'If ever you disturb our streets again, / Your lives shall pay the forfeit of the peace'. This serves to create a sense of foreboding and doom.

(c) The vulgar jokes of the Capulet servants, written in prose rather than verse, initially suggested to me that the feud was more ridiculous than serious and that the young men had been caught up in nothing more than silly shows of bravado. The hatred of Tybalt, contrasting sharply with the peaceful character of Benvolio, made me suspect that love and hate would be central themes in the play. Capulet and Montague seemed equally foolish when they needed to be restrained by their wives. Lady Capulet's sarcastic comment that a 'crutch' would be more fitting for Capulet than a 'sword' and Lady Montague's determination that her husband 'shalt not stir a foot to seek a foe', made me think that the women were more sensible than the men and perhaps would be able to assert some control over the situation. However, the Prince, speaking in lofty blank verse, impressed me the most with his determination to restore the peace of Verona, even if that meant imposing the death penalty on future offenders. When Romeo entered the scene after the brawl, his disinterest in the feud was remarkable. I was intrigued by his attitude and wondered how the disturbances on the streets of Verona would have an impact on his life.

4. Character

A character is an imaginary person in a narrative. In a play a character can be static (unchanging) or dynamic (capable of change). The main character in a play is called the **protagonist**, while the person opposing them or hostile to them is called the **antagonist**.

When discussing characters in a scene you should ask yourself:

(a) What are they doing?

(b) What are they saying?

(c) How are they speaking (diction and tone of voice)?

(d) How do they relate to other characters?

(e) How do they change or develop in the extract?

(f) What motivates their actions and words?

(g) Do you like or dislike a character? Why or why not?

(h) What impression do you form of a character and why?

When you are writing about characters, do not fall into the trap of telling the story of the extract or summarising what a character says or does. You must **analyse** each of the above questions (a)–(h) and make points which you can support from the text. Your task is to show that you can **interpret and form opinions** about the characters, their motives and their relationships.

The following extract is from Shakespeare's play *The Tempest*.

Background information

This scene is set on a ship at sea. A terrible storm is raging and a tempestuous noise of thunder and lightning is heard. The ship's master (the Captain) and the boatswain (the officer in charge of the ship's sails and rigging) are struggling in difficult circumstances to keep the ship afloat and to save the important passengers and the mariners (sailors) from drowning.

SCENE I. On a ship at sea: a tempestuous noise of thunder and lightning heard.

Enter a Master and a Boatswain

MASTER

Boatswain!

BOATSWAIN

Here, master: what cheer?

MASTER

Good, speak to the mariners: fall to't, yarely*,
or we run ourselves aground: bestir, bestir.

Exit.

Enter Mariners

BOATSWAIN

Heigh, my hearts! cheerly, cheerly, my hearts!
yare, yare! Take in the topsail. Tend to the master's whistle.
Blow, till thou burst thy wind,
if room enough!

Enter ALONSO, SEBASTIAN, ANTONIO, FERDINAND, GONZALO, and others

ALONSO

Good boatswain, have care. Where's the master?
Play the men.

BOATSWAIN

I pray now, keep below.

ANTONIO

Where is the master, boatswain?

BOATSWAIN

Do you not hear him? You mar our labour: keep your
cabins: you do assist the storm.

GONZALO

Nay, good*, be patient.

BOATSWAIN

When the sea is. Hence! What cares these roarers*
for the name of king? To cabin: silence! trouble us not.

GONZALO

Good, yet remember whom thou hast aboard.

BOATSWAIN

None that I more love than myself. You are a
counsellor; if you can command these elements to silence,
and work the peace of the present, we will
not hand a rope more; use your authority: if you cannot, give
thanks you have lived so long, and make
yourself ready in your cabin for the mischance
of the hour, if it so hap*. Cheerly, good hearts! Out
of our way, I say.

Exit Boatswain

GONZALO

I have great comfort from this fellow: methinks
he hath no drowning mark upon him; his complexion is
perfect gallows. If he be not born to be hanged, our case is
miserable.

Re-enter Boatswain

BOATSWAIN

Down with the topmast! yare! lower, lower!
Bring her to try with main-course.

A cry within

A plague upon this howling! they are louder than the weather
or our office.

Re-enter SEBASTIAN, ANTONIO, and GONZALO

Yet again! what do you here? Shall we give o'er
and drown? Have you a mind to sink?

SEBASTIAN

A pox o' your throat, you bawling, blasphemous,
incharitable dog!

BOATSWAIN

Work you then.

ANTONIO

Hang, cur! hang, you whoreson, insolent noisemaker!
We are less afraid to be drowned than thou art.

GONZALO

I'll warrant him for drowning; though the ship were no stronger than a nutshell.

BOATSWAIN

Lay her a-hold, a-hold! set her two courses off to sea again; lay her off.

Enter Mariners wet

MARINERS

All lost! to prayers, to prayers! all lost!

yarely = briskly, quickly

good = good fellow

roarers = roaring waves

hap = happen

Questions

?

1. (a) What is the boatswain doing in this extract? □

   A. He is trying to steady the ship in the storm.

   B. He is trying to irritate the passengers by giving orders.

   C. He is showing off his control of the ship.

   (b) How is he speaking to the passengers? □

   A. He is speaking aggressively and rudely.

   B. He is speaking plainly and with urgency.

   C. He is speaking humbly to the nobles.

   (c) What motivates the boatswain's actions and words? □

   A. He is determined to insult the noble passengers on board.

   B. He is motivated by a desire to please his master.

   C. He is motivated by a desire to save his own life and that of others.

   (d) What type of language is spoken by the boatswain? □

   A. Blank Verse

   B. Prose

   C. Rhyming couplets

2. What impression of the boatswain do you form from your reading of this extract? Support your answer with reference to the text.

3. **Making Connections:** From a Shakespearean play which you have studied, select a character who dominated (had the strongest presence in) a scene. Briefly describe the setting, atmosphere and action in this scene, showing how your impression of the character was shaped by his/her words and actions.

Tip:
When answering a question which asks you to form an impression of a character, use the PQE format
- Point
- Quotation to support point
- Explanation of point

Sample Question and Answer on Character

2. **What impression of the boatswain do you form from your reading of this extract? Support your answer with reference to the text.**

I get the impression that the boatswain is an experienced and skilful sailor. He is courageous and refuses to be intimidated by either the storm or the importance of his royal passengers. [Points stated in opening]

His experience and skill are apparent in the way he calmly deals with the situation. [Point] He does not panic but gives orders firmly: 'yare, yare! Take in the topsail.' He orders the mariners to lower the topmast, emphasising the importance of speed. Although he is insulted by Antonio, who calls him a 'cur' and a 'noisemaker', he keeps his mind on the task of steadying the ship and maintains control in a confident way. [Quotations and support from text to explain point]

The impression is clearly given of a man who is courageous and outspoken. [Point] When most of the passengers and even the other mariners are panicking, the boatswain shows very little fear. He confronts the storm by telling it to 'Blow, till thou burst thy wind!' He will not allow the passengers, regardless of their importance, to 'assist the storm' by coming on deck and orders them to return to their cabins: 'To cabin! silence! trouble us not!' He reminds the nobles that the 'roarers' have no respect for titles or 'the name of king'. [Quotations and explanation of point]

Although the other characters seem to have little faith in the boatswain, I get the clear impression that he is a capable individual who takes his duties seriously and who will 'command' the elements and restore 'peace'. [Conclusion addresses question and offers further quotation as support]

Conflict

When discussing character it is important to remember that **there is no drama without conflict**. The conflict or opposing forces in a play can be external (between characters) or internal (within a character) and is usually resolved by the end of the play. Incidents involving conflict or contrast give us a deeper insight into characters.

The following extract (in edited form) is adapted from Shakespeare's comedy, *As You Like It*. Read the extract carefully and then answer the questions which follow.

Background information

Silvius, a shepherd living in the Forest of Arden, is in love with Phebe – a dark-haired, beautiful young woman, who does not return his love. In this scene Phebe has just rejected Silvius. Rosalind is a young noble woman who has been banished from court. Disguised as a man, she seeks refuge, also in the Forest of Arden, where she eavesdrops on an argument between Silvius and Phebe. She decides to get involved!

SILVIUS
Sweet Phebe, do not scorn me; do not, Phebe;
Say that you love me not, but say not so
In bitterness.
The common executioner,
Whose heart th'accustomed sight of death makes hard,
Falls not the axe upon the humbled neck
But first begs pardon: will you sterner be
Than he that dies and lives by bloody drops?

[Rosalind enters unnoticed]

PHEBE
I would not be thy executioner:
I fly thee, but I would not injure thee.
Thou tell'st me there is murder in mine eye:
If mine eyes can wound, now let them kill thee:
But show me the wound mine eye hath made in thee!
Scratch thee but with a pin, and there remains
Some scar of it; but now mine eyes,
Which I have darted at thee, hurt thee not,
Nor, I am sure, there is no force in eyes
That can do hurt.

SILVIUS

O dear Phebe,

If ever – as that ever may be near –
You meet in some fresh cheek the power of fancy,
Then shall you know the wounds invisible
That love's keen arrows make.

PHEBE

But till that time

Come not thou near me: and when that time comes,
Afflict me with thy mocks, pity me not;
As till that time I shall not pity thee.

ROSALIND

Coming forward

And why, I pray you? Who might be your mother,
That you insult the wretched?
What though you have no beauty–
As by my faith, I see no more in you
Than without candle may go dark to bed –
Must you be therefore proud and pitiless?
Why, what means this? Why do you look on me?
I see no more in you than in the ordinary
Of nature's sale-work – God save my little life,
I think she means to tangle my eyes too!
No, faith, proud mistress, hope not after it:
'Tis not your inky brows, your black silk hair,
Your bugle eyeballs, nor your cheek of cream,
That can entrance my spirits to your worship.
You foolish shepherd, wherefore do you follow her,
Like foggy south, puffing with wind and rain?
You are a thousand times a properer man
Than she a woman: 'tis such fools as you
That makes the world full of ill-favoured children:
'Tis not her glass*, but you, that flatters her;
And out of you she sees herself more proper
Than any of her features can show her.
But, mistress, know yourself: down on your knees,
And thank heaven, fasting, for a good man's love:
For I must tell you friendly in your ear,
Sell when you can: you are not for all markets:
Cry the man mercy; love him; take his offer:
Take her to thee, shepherd: Fare you well.

PHEBE

to Rosalind

Sweet youth, I pray you, chide* a year together:
I had rather hear you chide than this man woo.

glass = mirror
chide = scold

Questions

1. Compare the characters of Silvius and Phebe as revealed in the opening speeches of this extract. Support your answer with reference to the extract up to the point when Rosalind speaks.

2. Which of the two women characters in the above extract is the more appealing in your opinion? Give reasons for your answer.

3. Write stage directions for the actor playing the part of Rosalind to follow when she is delivering her speeches. Explain how your stage directions would help to heighten the effect of what Rosalind is saying. Support your answer with reference to the scene.

4. What do you think Rosalind means when she advises Phebe to 'Sell when you can: you are not for all markets'?

5. Taking into consideration the words spoken by Phebe at the end of this scene, what do you predict will happen later between her and Rosalind?

6. Which of the following terms describes the form of the above speeches (a) prose, (b) blank verse, (c) rhymed verse? Give a clear reason for your answer.

7. Basing your answer on the above extract and the background information, discuss what aspects of the play are captured in this poster for a production of *As You Like It*?

8. **Making connections:** Select a scene or extract from a Shakespearean play you have studied where two characters have an episode of conflict. Explain how this conflict arose and what it revealed about the characters involved.

Poster Design © 2014 David Zinn

Tip:

For Studied Drama, you will be expected to have studied the main characters in considerable depth. Ask yourself the questions (a) – (h) on page 33 about the characters and be very clear about how each character's actions influence the plot and themes of the play.

- Be prepared to **discuss the main characters,** showing an awareness of their personalities, strengths, weaknesses, motivations and roles in the plot. Decide what you **admire or dislike** about each of them. Have **quotations** prepared to **support your points**.

- You should also be able to explore the **conflicts** between characters in the play. Know **how and why** these conflicts arise, how they **develop** in the course of the play and how they **resolve**. Have **key scenes** prepared in some detail so that you can illustrate **major moments of conflict**.

- Be ready to discuss the way **characters are contrasted** throughout the play. Be able to show the **effect** of the contrasts and how they **add to our understanding** of the play.

- Be prepared to discuss the use of **language and dialogue** in revealing characters.

5. Plot

The plot is the sequence of events in the story. You should pay careful attention to each of the following questions:

(a) Is there any **conflict, suspense or tension** in this extract / scene? Where? Why?

(b) Is the conflict meant to be **serious or comic** in its effect on the audience?

(c) Does tension **build up**? How does it build up?

(d) Does tension reach a **climax**? Where?

(e) Does the tension **relax** in the extract / scene? Where and how does it relax?

(f) Does anything happen which has an **impact on the plot**?

(g) What might happen next?

(h) Is there any underlying **message or theme** in the extract?

For the Studied Drama questions:

- Ensure that you know the **full story** of the play and the **sequence of events**.

- Be prepared to show how **certain major events** create a **change** in the **direction of the plot**. For example, by killing Tybalt in revenge for Mercutio's death, Romeo, in *Romeo and Juliet*, becomes an exile in Mantua – something which contributes to the disastrous ending. Similarly, in *As You Like It*, a true turning point is when Oliver and Celia fall in love, which makes Orlando want to abandon the game with Ganymede and seek the 'real' Rosalind. This influences Rosalind's decision to marry him the next day.

- It is very advisable to create a **timeline of events** for the play you have chosen to study. Clearly **highlight the turning points** or **major events** and be aware of **how** each one influences the plot.

- Be prepared to show your understanding of how the plot **opens, develops, reaches a climax and resolves**.

Important terms for Shakespearean drama

Act:	A major division in a play. An act is sub-divided into scenes.
Antagonist:	A character or force against which another character struggles.
Aside:	Words spoken by a character directly to the audience, but not heard by the other characters on the stage.
Climax:	The turning point of the plot and the point of greatest tension.
Comedy:	A play in which the main character/s triumph over obstacles and negative circumstances, and achieve a happy conclusion.
Conflict:	The struggle between opposing forces. There is no drama without conflict.
Complication:	An intensification of the conflict in a play – Act II is known as the complication.
Dialogue:	The conversation between characters.
Dynamic Character:	A character who changes or develops in the course of the play.
Exit:	A character leaves the stage.
Exeunt:	More than one character leaves the stage.
Gesture:	A physical movement made by a character during a play.
Monologue:	A speech made by a single character without another character's response.
Motivation:	An idea or thought that drives a character to achieve a goal.
Plot:	The sequence of events that make up a story.
Props:	Articles or objects that appear on stage during a play.
Protagonist:	The main character. (In some plays, like *Romeo and Juliet*, there is more than one protagonist.)
Scene:	A portion or segment of an act which indicates changes of location or time, introduces new character/s or provides a movement from one plot to another.
Scenery:	The physical representation of the play's setting (location and time period).
Static Character:	A character who does not change or develop in the course of the play.
Soliloquy:	A speech which is heard by the audience but not by other characters on the stage. It reveals the private thoughts of the character.
Tragedy:	A type of play in which the protagonist and other characters experience loss and suffering. Tragedies usually involve the death of the main character and others.

C. Key Skills for Analysing Modern Drama

All the skills required for engaging and responding to Shakespearean drama apply to modern drama. What we have already learnt about setting, atmosphere, characterisation, plot development, etc. are also major features to consider when discussing modern extracts and plays.

Some obvious differences are:

- Most modern plays are written mainly in **prose** rather than in blank or rhymed verse.
- The **language used is easier** for a modern audience to read and understand.
- Modern plays are **more realistic** than Shakespearean plays.
- **Stage directions** are usually **more detailed** in modern plays.
- The audience is not as dependant on the dialogue to establish setting or time.
- **Stagecraft has more advanced techniques available** – impressive effects can be created using modern technology.
- Clever **use of lighting** can focus the attention of the audience on a character or location and can also differentiate scenes taking place at night from those occurring in daylight.

1. More about Stage Directions

In a play, stage directions are **instructions from the playwright** to the actors and stage crew. These directions are often placed within brackets and are not communicated to the audience. From your reading of extracts and full texts of modern plays, you will be very familiar with the appearance of these directions.

Stage directions allow the playwright to communicate his/her intentions for actors' entrances, exits, movements, tone of voice and facial expressions. In addition, they provide guidance for the stage crew regarding their backstage duties, such as lighting and changes of lighting, sound effects, background music or anything else that needs to be added. They also can be used to provide information about what is happening in the background, away from the main action, for example, *a roll of thunder is heard in the distance.*

Stage directions on how actors should speak are inserted in brackets, usually at the beginning of lines, unless the tone changes in the course of what is being said. For example, words like *sadly, threateningly, furiously, timidly,* etc. are often put at the start of the line.

Directions that are specifically intended for the stage crew, such as, *a bell rings,* are usually separated from dialogue and placed on their own lines. They are sometimes, but not always, placed within brackets.

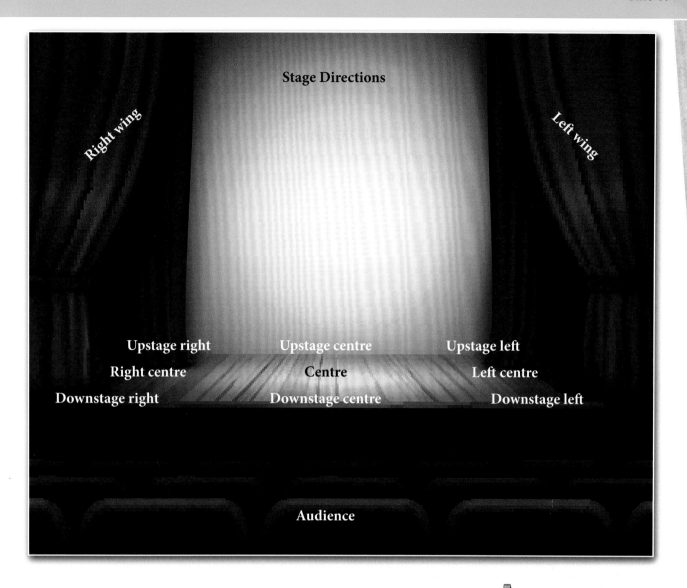

An important function for stage directions is to tell the actors their positions on stage. **Downstage** is at the front, near the audience and **upstage** is at the back. **Centre stage** is between the two. In addition, **left** and **right** refer to the actors' positions when they are facing the audience. For example, when actors walk **stage right**, they are moving to the audience's left side.

The diagram above makes these positions clear.

2. Modern Tragedy

Modern plays are not usually divided into tragedies or comedies in the same way as Shakespearean plays are.

While Shakespeare's tragic heroes are **socially important people** who are flawed and who often bring their disasters upon themselves, **modern tragedy** places **ordinary people** in dreadful situations, which are not always of their own making.

Read the following extract which is taken from the tragic play *Riders to the Sea* by J. M. Synge.

Background information

Maurya has lost her husband and five of her sons to the sea. As the play begins, her daughters, Nora and Cathleen, receive word from a priest that a body, which may be their brother Michael, has been found further north on a shore in Donegal. Their other brother, Bartley, has just left home to bring horses to a fair in Galway.

Scene 1.

[*An island off the West of Ireland. Cottage kitchen, with nets, oilskins, spinning-wheel, some new boards standing by the wall, etc. CATHLEEN, a girl of about 20, finishes kneading cake, and puts it down in the pot-oven by the fire; then wipes her hands, and begins to spin at the wheel. NORA, a young girl, puts her head in at the door.*]

NORA: (*in a low voice*) Where is she?

CATHLEEN: She's lying down, God help her, and maybe sleeping, if she's able.

[*NORA comes in softly, and takes a bundle from under her shawl.*]

CATHLEEN: (*spinning the wheel rapidly*) What is it you have?

NORA: The young priest is after bringing them. It's a shirt and a plain stocking were got off a drowned man in Donegal.

[*CATHLEEN stops her wheel with a sudden movement, and leans out to listen.*]

NORA: We're to find out if it's Michael's they are; some time herself will be down looking by the sea.

CATHLEEN: How would they be Michael's, Nora? How would he go the length of that way to the far north?

NORA: The young priest says he's known the like of it. "If it's Michael's they are," says he, "you can tell herself he's got a clean burial by the grace of God, and if they're not his, let no one say a word about them, for she'll be getting her death," says he, "with crying and lamenting."

[*The door which NORA half closed is blown open by a gust of wind.*]

CATHLEEN: (*looking out anxiously*) Did you ask him would he stop Bartley going this day with the horses to the Galway fair?

NORA: "I won't stop him," says he, "but let you not be afraid. Herself does be saying prayers half through the night, and the Almighty God won't leave her destitute," says he, "with no son living."

CATHLEEN: Is the sea bad by the white rocks, Nora?

NORA: Middling bad, God help us. There's a great roaring in the west, and it's worse it'll be getting when the tide's turned to the wind.

[*She goes over to the table with the bundle.*]

Shall I open it now?

CATHLEEN: Maybe she'd wake up on us, and come in before we'd done.

[*Coming to the table*]

It's a long time we'll be, and the two of us crying.

NORA: (*goes to the inner door and listens*) She's moving about on the bed. She'll be coming in a minute.

CATHLEEN: Give me the ladder, and I'll put them up in the turf-loft, the way she won't know of them at all, and maybe when the tide turns she'll be going down to see would he be floating from the east.

[*They put the ladder against the gable of the chimney;
CATHLEEN goes up a few steps and hides the bundle in the turf-loft.
MAURYA comes from the inner room.*]

MAURYA: (*looking up at CATHLEEN and speaking querulously*) Isn't it turf enough you have for this day and evening?

CATHLEEN: There's a cake baking at the fire for a short space (*throwing down the turf*) and Bartley will want it when the tide turns if he goes to Connemara.

[*NORA picks up the turf and puts it round the pot-oven.*]

Questions

1. From the description of the setting (at the opening of the scene) and from the given stage directions, make a list of all the props which would need to be assembled before staging this extract.

2. Draw a sketch of the stage indicating where you would place doors, windows, the loft and all of the essential props to create the setting.

3. How does the playwright suggest the location and the time of the action in the extract?

4. How is tension created in the extract? Support your answer with evidence from the text.

5. What type of clothing would be worn by the characters in the extract? Explain your choices.

6. If you were directing this scene, what sound and lighting effects could you use to highlight the setting and the action.

7. What impression do you get of the relationships between Nora, Cathleen and Maurya? Explain your answer with support from the text.

8. Imagine that you are a reporter from a Donegal newspaper. Write a short news report about the discovery of the man's body on the shore.

9. Explain the meaning of the following words as used in the above extract: gust, destitute, querulously. Write a sentence for each word which clearly indicates its meaning.

10. Cathleen says of Maurya that, 'maybe when the tide turns she'll be going down to see would he be floating from the east'. This suggests that Maurya already knows that Michael has drowned, so why are her daughters hiding the bundle of clothes? Explain your response using details from the extract.

11. **Making Connections:** From a play which you have studied, select a scene where tension is created effectively. Explain what has happened just before the scene opens and what happens in the scene. Comment on the part played by stage directions in creating the tense atmosphere.

3. Modern Comedy

A modern **comedy** refers to a play which is designed to arouse laughter and which does not end in disaster but shows characters overcoming obstacles. Certain types of comedy involve intellectual wit and are often set among high society; characterisations are clever and the plot reveals complex situations. An element of **farce** is often introduced, where **hyperbole** (exaggeration) and extreme characters are placed in absurd circumstances that seem to spiral out of control. An example of this type of comedy is *The Importance of Being Earnest* and other plays by Oscar Wilde.

Satires are comedies where society or politics are mocked and criticised.

Not every modern play falls neatly into the category of a tragedy or comedy. Many plays have elements of both comedy and tragedy, in which case they are referred to as **tragi-comedy**. Some plays defy any classification.

The following extract from Oscar Wilde's play *The Importance of Being Earnest* is an example of comic farce.

Background information

Lady Bracknell, the mother of a young lady named Gwendolen, interrogates a young man called Jack to determine his suitability to marry her daughter. When Jack explains that he was found in a handbag abandoned in a railway station, Lady Bracknell is horrified.

LADY BRACKNELL
. . . Now to minor matters. Are your parents living?

JACK
I have lost both my parents.

LADY BRACKNELL
To lose one parent, Mr Worthing, may be regarded as a misfortune; to lose both looks like carelessness. Who was your father? He was evidently a man of some wealth. Was he born in what the Radical papers call the purple of commerce, or did he rise from the ranks of aristocracy?

JACK
I am afraid I really don't know. The fact is, Lady Bracknell, I said I had lost my parents. It would be nearer the truth to say that my parents seem to have lost me . . . I don't actually know who I am by birth. I was . . . well, I was found.

LADY BRACKNELL
Found!

JACK
The late Mr. Thomas Cardew, an old gentleman of a very charitable and kindly disposition, found me, and gave me the name of Worthing, because he happened to have a first-class ticket for Worthing in his pocket at the time. Worthing is a place in Sussex. It is a seaside resort.

LADY BRACKNELL
Where did the charitable gentleman who had a first-class ticket for this seaside resort find you?

JACK
[*Gravely*] In a hand-bag.

LADY BRACKNELL
A hand-bag?

JACK

[*Very seriously*] Yes, Lady Bracknell. I was in a hand-bag – a somewhat large, black leather hand-bag, with handles to it – an ordinary hand-bag, in fact.

LADY BRACKNELL

In what locality did this Mr. James, or Thomas, Cardew come across this ordinary hand-bag?

JACK

In the cloak-room at Victoria Station. It was given to him in mistake for his own.

LADY BRACKNELL

The cloak-room at Victoria Station?

JACK

Yes. The Brighton Line.

LADY BRACKNELL

The line is immaterial. Mr. Worthing, I confess I feel somewhat bewildered by what you have just told me. To be born, or at any rate, bred in a hand-bag, whether it had handles or not, seems to me to display a contempt for the ordinary decencies of family life that remind one of the worst excesses of the French Revolution. And I presume you know what that unfortunate movement led to? As for the particular locality in which the hand-bag was found, a cloak-room at a railway station might serve to conceal a social indiscretion – has probably, indeed, been used for that purpose before now – but it could hardly be regarded as an assured basis for a recognised position in good society.

JACK

May I ask you then what you would advise me to do? I need hardly say I would do anything in the world to ensure Gwendolen's happiness.

LADY BRACKNELL

I would strongly advise you, Mr. Worthing, to try and acquire some relations as soon as possible, and to make a definite effort to produce at any rate one parent, of either sex, before the season is quite over.

JACK

Well, I don't see how I could possibly manage to do that. I can produce the hand-bag at any moment. It is in my dressing-room at home. I really think that should satisfy you, Lady Bracknell.

LADY BRACKNELL

Me, sir! What has it to do with me? You can hardly imagine that I and Lord Bracknell would dream of allowing our only daughter – a girl brought up with the utmost care – to marry into a cloak-room, and form an alliance with a parcel? Good morning, Mr. Worthing!

[*Lady Bracknell sweeps out in majestic indignation.*]

Questions

1. Exaggeration, or hyperbole, is used effectively for comic purpose in the extract. Select three examples and explain how each adds to the humour.
2. Some aspects of society are satirised in the extract. What are these aspects in your opinion? Explain and support your answer.
3. Add three extra stage directions to the script and explain how each would add to the creation of the comedy.
4. If you were directing this scene what gestures and facial expressions would you suggest for each of Lady Bracknell's reactions to Jack's admission that he was 'found'? Explain your response.
5. What does Lady Bracknell mean when she says, 'To lose one parent, Mr Worthing, may be regarded as a misfortune; to lose both looks like carelessness'?

A type of comedy using clownish or silly antics to create fun is referred to as **slapstick**.

This type of comedy is based on deliberately clumsy actions and gets its name from a device where two pieces of wood were joined together and used to make a loud slapping noise. Pantomimes often use slapstick.

Background information

This extract is adapted from the play *Alphabetical Order* by Michael Frayn.

Lucy works in the library of a provincial newspaper. It is her job to cut out and file extracts from a variety of newspapers for reference purposes. The other characters in this extract (Wally, John, Nora, Geoffrey and Lesley) are Lucy's colleagues. They also work for the newspaper.

In this scene one of the journalists, Wally, has cut his hand and comes to Lucy for assistance.

LUCY
(lacklustre) What do you want now, Wally?

WALLY
I've got a ladder outside the window.

GEOFFREY
That's right, Wally. You cheer her up.

WALLY
Where's the horse?

LUCY
He can't hear you.

WALLY

The horse is holding the ladder. Right? Right! Off we go. Oh – just one thing.

(He whips away the handkerchief he is holding,
and reveals that the hand is injured.)

LUCY

Oh my God! What happened?

WALLY

Where do you want me to bleed? Over *The Times* or the *Guardian?*

LUCY

Hold on. I'll get the first-aid box.

GEOFFREY

Lucy'll soon have that bandaged up for you.

NORA

Have you washed it?

WALLY

I don't know. I was just quietly putting my hand into the jeweller's window
. . .

NORA

Washed it. Have you washed it?

WALLY

Actually I was just quietly punching the Editor on the nose . . .

GEOFFREY

Here she comes, the Lady with the Lamp.

JOHN

A miracle she hasn't lost the first-aid box.

LUCY

But . . . the key . . .

JOHN

And she's lost the key!

NORA

Oh dear. Lucy.

(Lucy, Geoffrey, John and Nora and Arnold all search urgently.
Wally waits patiently. Lesley watches them all.)

LUCY

Everyone was helping themselves.

JOHN
She's locked the first-aid box, and she's lost the key!

LUCY
It was my one bit of efficiency.

NORA
Oh dear, this could be rather serious.

WALLY
Would you like me to die in here, or shall I go outside?

JOHN
(to the world at large) We've got the box. But we can't open it.

NORA
This really is one of our less appealing muddles.

LUCY
Well you look after it! I don't want to do it!

GEOFFREY
Now let's all keep calm.

LUCY
I always get landed with these rotten jobs that no one else wants!

JOHN
Hadn't we better discuss the injustice of the world later?

LUCY
Do the collections for farewell presents. Run the Christmas raffle. Sell the tickets for the staff dance. Help with the children's treat . . . And I haven't got any children! I hate children!

NORA
No, you don't . . .

LUCY
Yes, I do! I hate their parents, too! And I'm sick of being nice! Everyone takes it for granted I'm nice, and I'm not, and I'm fed up of pretending to be! I'm also fed up with the effort of thinking everyone else is nice! I'm worn out with the sheer hard labour of seeing any sense in anything!

JOHN
Sit down.

GEOFFREY
Take a deep breath.

LUCY

I sit here all day keeping nothingness stuck together by sheer effort of will. And what happens? I lose the only thing that really matters! Now I have to watch Wally stand there and bleed to death!

JOHN

He's not bleeding to death.

WALLY

It is you know. It's running up my sleeve.

LUCY

I'm sorry, Wally! I'm sorry! I've come over all to pieces! I don't know what I'm doing!

(Lesley comes forward holding the leg of the broken chair, and opens the first-aid box with a single sharp blow. Silence.)

GEOFFREY

Well, that's one way of doing it.

LESLEY

Sorry. I thought probably we'd better not wait for the key. Sorry.

(Lucy dresses Wally's hand.)

Questions

1. What impression of Lucy do you form from reading this extract? Support your answer with reference to the extract.

2. Would you describe this extract as being purely slapstick with no serious element at all? Explain why or why not.

3. What do you think Lucy means when she says, 'I sit here all day keeping nothingness stuck together by sheer effort of will'?

4. Imagine that you are Wally. Write an email to Lucy, thanking her for her assistance and commenting on the behaviour of the other office workers.

5. You have decided to audition for a part in your school's production of *Alphabetical Order*. Based on your reading of the above extract, which part would you most like to play? Explain your answer.

Sample Questions and Answers on an Unseen Extract

When answering questions based on an extract, use the PQE method as indicated in the sample answer to Q.1. This will give your answer a clear structure.

1. **What impression of Lucy do you form from reading this extract? Support your answer with reference to the extract.**

    From reading this extract, I get the impression that Lucy is a bit of a scatterbrain who resents the fact that she is taken for granted by her colleagues. She seems to be completely overwhelmed by her many and varied duties. **[P]**

    I can tell that Lucy is disorganised **[P]** because John sarcastically remarks that it is 'A miracle she hasn't lost the first-aid box' and also points out that Lucy has 'lost the key'. Lucy herself acknowledges she is a bit scattered and inefficient by admitting that looking after the box was her 'one bit of efficiency'. **[Q + E]**

    It is clear from the extract that Lucy resents being taken for granted by others. **[P]** She complains that she always gets 'landed' with the 'rotten jobs that no one else wants'. She becomes self-pitying and sulky when listing all the jobs she undertakes. This makes me wonder why she accepts these responsibilities in the first place. Perhaps she is just trying to be 'nice' and has now become 'sick of being nice'. Her resentment sounds slightly childish when she says 'Well you look after it! I don't want to do it!' **[Q + E]**

    There is no doubt that Lucy feels overwhelmed. **[P]** She appears to become hysterical when she uses phrases like 'I'm sick of...' 'I'm fed up of...', 'I'm worn out...' and ends up by telling Wally that she has '...come over all to pieces! I don't know what I'm doing!' Her tendency to be melodramatic is obvious when she thinks she has to 'watch Wally bleed to death'. **[Q + E]**

    Overall, I get the impression that Lucy has taken on too many responsibilities for such an inefficient, highly strung person. **[Conclusion]**

2. **There are many elements that help to make this passage an entertaining piece of drama. In your opinion, what are these elements?**

    There are several elements which help to make this an entertaining piece of drama. In my opinion, comedy is created in the situation, in the dialogue and in the characterisation.

    The lost key results in an entertaining reaction from Lucy, who blows the situation out of all proportion to its real importance. Wally is certainly not 'bleeding to death' and if he were, they would need much more than a 'first-aid box'! The situation has many elements of slapstick comedy. Wally's dramatic whipping away of the handkerchief to reveal his cut hand and the frantic search for the key are funny. The problem is resolved in typical slapstick fashion when the box is broken open with the leg of the chair. Stage directions helped me to visualise the scene and be amused by it.

Comedy is also created in the use of dialogue. Wally asks Lucy if she wants him to bleed 'Over *The Times* or the *Guardian*', while John keeps up a running commentary on Lucy's incompetence – 'She's locked the first-aid box, and she's lost the key!' The one line spoken by Lesley at the end of the passage is very funny as she apologises for smashing open the box – 'Sorry. I thought probably we'd better not wait for the key. Sorry'. I enjoyed the dialogue immensely and was very entertained by it.

All of the characters are entertaining in different ways. Lucy in her hysterical reaction and bubbling resentment, Wally in his dramatic gestures, John in his role as judge of Lucy's efficiency and his biting sarcasm. The other characters, Nora and Geoffrey, are more calm and balanced in their response. Nora keeps saying 'Oh dear', while Geoffrey appeals for calm – 'Now let's all keep calm' and advises Lucy to 'Take a deep breath'. This contrast between the characters serves to highlight the exaggeration of the pretended conflict in the situation. The silent, practical Lesley provides a very comic moment when, after a dramatic pause, he suddenly takes things into his own hands and, with apologies, smashes the box open.

In my opinion, the writer creates entertainment by blending characters, situation and dialogue in a very clever and amusing way.

4. Atmosphere, Tension and Conflict

Atmosphere or **mood** is the feeling or tone created in a scene. It is often created through a combination of several dramatic and stagecraft elements working together. For example, mood can be created through sound, lighting, movement, setting, rhythm, contrast, tension and conflict.

Tension refers to the development of **suspense** in a performance. As the audience anticipates certain outcomes in the plot, the tension builds. An obvious example of rising tension is in a mystery or detective story. The development of tension usually parallels the advancement of the plot, leading to a **crisis** or **climax**. The extract from *Riders to the Sea* has a tense atmosphere due to the circumstances of a family death. As the play progresses, tension builds up, reaches a climax and finally reaches a **resolution**.

Conflict differs slightly from tension in that it is often related to characters who clash with one another rather than to circumstances alone. It can be **verbal** (using words), **physical** or **psychological**. This next extract is an example of a scene where conflict has arisen between two characters.

The following extract (slightly shortened) is taken from the play *The Granny Project* by Anne Fine.

Background information

Ivan, a teenage boy, has written a project for school which he has named 'The Granny Project'. In it, he describes very intimate details of his family life, particularly those concerning his grandmother, who is about to be sent into an old folks' home. His father, Henry, has just found and read 'The Granny Project'.

[Henry is standing behind the kitchen table on which the Granny Project lies like a trial exhibit. Ivan is standing in front.]

HENRY: This thing here. This— Granny Project. Well . . . ?

IVAN: Yes?

HENRY: I'm asking you!

IVAN: Well, I was going to hand it in on Monday.

HENRY: Is it a joke?

IVAN: No. Not a joke.

HENRY: Who chose this topic?

IVAN: It was Sophie's idea at the very start.

HENRY: I don't see Sophie's name on this.

IVAN: Sophie dropped out.

HENRY: Thought better of it you mean?

IVAN: Changed her mind, yes.

HENRY: And so it's all yours now. And what's it for?

IVAN: Well, it's for Social Science homework, in one sense . . .

HENRY: And in another . . .?

IVAN: I suppose, in another, you could say that it was blackmail.

HENRY: Blackmail?

IVAN: Blackmail. To stop you putting Granny into that Home.

HENRY: We keep your Granny here, or you hand this in at school.

IVAN: That's right.

HENRY: I see. Tell me, this thing, this vicious and disloyal document, this hurtful and insensitive catalogue of eavesdroppings – you don't feel this to be dishonourable?

IVAN: I feel it is, yes. But I don't think it is. With Sophie, the feelings took over. That's why she dropped out in the end. I reconsidered then. Of course I did. But still I thought that I was right, so I kept going.

HENRY: Ivan, it makes me ill to think a son of mine could act like this. That he could think this thing through in such a cold, inhuman fashion. You carry on this way and God knows what a barbarous mess you'll make of your life. You live in this house. You know what a strain it's been looking after my mother. Where's your sympathy, your understanding, your warmth? If you act this way in your own family, where do you think you will end up?

IVAN: Sophie thinks I'll be a revolutionary.

HENRY: You're not a grown-up revolutionary yet, you know. And I'm still your father. I could just burn this folder.

IVAN: I'm not playing games, Dad, I have copies.

HENRY: Ivan, I'm coming very close to hitting you – hard.

IVAN: That isn't going to help.

HENRY: I would feel better.

IVAN: Feelings, again.

HENRY: Get out! Get out of here! **Get out!**

Questions

?

1. What kind of relationship exists between Ivan and his father? Support your answer with references from the text.
2. Would you describe the conflict in this extract as being verbal, physical, psychological or a combination of all three? Explain your answer giving specific examples from the text.
3. How is the conflict in this scene different from the tension in the extract from *Riders to the Sea*? Explain your response.
4. You have been asked to write three stage directions into this script. What directions would you insert and where would you insert them? Give reasons for your choices.
5. Ivan says that Sophie, his sister, thinks that he will become a 'revolutionary'. Do you think that Ivan's behaviour justifies Sophie's opinion? Explain your response with reference to the text.
6. The background to this extract tells us that, Ivan 'describes very intimate details of his family life, particularly those concerning his grandmother, who is about

to be sent into an old folks' home'. Write out the text of one of Ivan's project entries, which has managed to infuriate his father.

7. **Making Connections:** Select a scene from a play which you have studied which shows conflict between two or more characters. Explain how and why this conflict arose and how it was resolved in the course of the play.

5. Changing Genre: Novel to Play

Many novels or short stories can be converted into playscripts by changing layout. The important things to remember when converting a short narrative extract into a dramatic scene are:

A.   Clearly indicate the different speakers' names at the left hand side of the page and use a colon after each name.

B.   Be selective in your choice of stage directions. Leave out anything which is not needed to move the story forward.

C.   Use the least amount of words possible and don't spend time describing action or setting. Only describe the things that can actually be SEEN or HEARD onstage.

D.   Good dialogue is found in quick back-and-forth exchanges rather than in long speeches.

The following extract is taken from John Steinbeck's novel *Of Mice and Men*. A playscript of this incident would retain the dialogue spoken by the characters, but **not the speech marks**. The narration would be replaced by stage directions.

For example, the opening lines:

> Curley stepped over to Lennie like a terrier. 'What the hell you laughin' at?'
> Lennie looked blankly at him. 'Huh?'
>
> Then Curley's rage exploded. 'Come on, ya big bastard. Get up on your feet.
> No big son-of-a-bitch is gonna laugh at me. I'll show ya who's yella.'

Becomes:

[Curley moves threateningly towards Lennie]

CURLEY: *(aggressively)* What the hell you laughin' at?

LENNIE: *(blankly)* Huh?

CURLEY: *(furiously)* Come on, ya big bastard. Get up on your feet. No big son-of-a-bitch is gonna laugh at me. I'll show ya who's yella.

Using the example on page 59 as a guide to layout, convert the remainder of this extract to a playscript.

Lennie looked helplessly at George, and then he got up and tried to retreat. Curley was balanced and poised. He slashed at Lennie with his left, and then smashed down his nose with a right. Lennie gave a cry of terror. Blood welled from his nose. 'George,' he cried. 'Make 'um let me alone, George.' He backed until he was against the wall, and Curley followed, slugging him in the face. Lennie's hands remained at his sides; he was too frightened to defend himself.

George was on his feet yelling, 'Get him, Lennie. Don't let him do it.'

Lennie covered his face with his huge paws and bleated with terror. He cried, 'Make 'um stop, George.' Then Curley attacked his stomach and cut off his wind.

Slim jumped up. 'The dirty little rat,' he cried, 'I'll get 'um myself.'

George put out his hand and grabbed Slim. 'Wait a minute,' he shouted. He cupped his hands around his mouth and yelled, 'Get 'im, Lennie!'

Lennie took his hands away from his face and looked about for George, and Curley slashed at his eyes. The big face was covered with blood. George yelled again, 'I said get him.'

Curley's fist was swinging when Lennie reached for it. The next minute Curley was flopping like a fish on a line, and his closed fist was lost in Lennie's big hand. George ran down the room. 'Leggo of him, Lennie. Let go.'

But Lennie watched in terror the flopping little man whom he held. Blood ran down Lennie's face, one of his eyes was cut and closed. George slapped him on the face again and again, and still Lennie held on to the closed fist. Curley was white and shrunken by now, and his struggling had become weak. He stood crying, his fist lost in Lennie's paw.

George shouted over and over, 'Leggo his hand, Lennie. Leggo. Slim, come help me while the guy got any hand left.'

Suddenly Lennie let go his hold. He crouched cowering against the wall. 'You tol' me to, George,' he said miserably.

Curley sat down on the floor, looking in wonder at his crushed hand. Slim and Carlson bent over him. Slim straightened up and regarded Lennie with horror. 'We got to get him in to a doctor,' he said. 'Looks to me like ever' bone in his han' is bust.'

'I didn't wanta,' Lennie cried. 'I didn't wanta hurt him.'

Extra Literary Terms

Important terms for modern drama

Farce:	A comedy based on absurd events.
Hyperbole:	Exaggeration, often for comic effect.
Slapstick:	Comedy based on deliberately clumsy actions and /or embarrassing events.
Tragi-comedy:	A play which has both elements of tragedy and comedy.

Use the following checklist to ensure that you have complied with the demands of the marking scheme:

1. Have I practised writing both unseen and studied questions on drama? ☐

2. Have I prepared my texts carefully following the guidelines for analysing drama? ☐

3. Have I read the questions very carefully and ensured that I am addressing all parts of the questions? ☐

4. Have I underlined the key words in all questions before choosing a question to answer? ☐

5. Have I made a short plan, ensuring that I am addressing the question? ☐

6. Have I made relevant points and supported them with quotation? ☐

7. Have I offered some explanation of my points? ☐

8. Have I made some personal comments in the course of my answer? ☐

9. Have I paragraphed properly, developing one point in each paragraph? ☐

10. Have I checked my spelling, punctuation and grammar? ☐

If you can tick each of these boxes, you will be able to answer questions on both unseen and studied drama.

02 Poetry

Learning Outcomes

This section addresses the following learning outcomes:
OL8, 12, R1– 9; W1, 3, 7, 8, 9.

Introduction

In your Final Assessment Examination, you may be required to answer questions on **unseen poetry** and **studied poetry**. You will need to have studied a wide variety of poems and understand the various **techniques** used by poets. You will also need to be able to link an unseen poem with a poem or poems which you have studied in class.

The exam questions will test your ability to **understand**, **respond** to and **analyse** the techniques used by the poet. You may be required to **compare and contrast** two different poems and/or offer suggestions relating to the drafting of a poem which you might consider writing yourself. The questions will be worth different marks, so pay careful attention to what each one gets and the amount of space that is provided for answers in your answer book. These will guide you as regards the length of your responses.

Key Skills for Answering on Poetry:

1. **Content**. You must **answer the questions** asked and **support your answers** with relevant quotation where appropriate.

2. **Structure**. You must structure your answer in an intelligent way. **Organise** your responses into paragraphs. Develop one major point in each paragraph. Use **varied sentence structures**.

3. **Expression**. You should be able to express yourself with **clarity and fluency**.

4. **Mechanics**. Spelling, punctuation and grammar are important in everything that you write. Always check these areas for total accuracy.

A. Key Skills for Reading and Responding to a Poem

In responding to poetry questions you must display an ability to connect with the poem and the poet. You are expected to make **intelligent use of the text of the poem to support your interpretation.** A knowledge of the following key terms is essential for understanding how to read and respond to a poem:

1. Language
2. Sound
3. Subject matter and theme
4. Tone
5. Point of view
6. Imagery

1. Language

You should be able to comment on the **word choices** made by the poet. A word can have a literal meaning, which is known as its *denotation.* The denotation of a word can be found in a dictionary. However, poets are more interested in the **connotations** of words. This refers to the **associations** which words can have. Take for example the word '*Fire*' – what associations can be made with this word?

Clever choices and combinations of words create layers of meaning in a poem. Be on the lookout for unusual or striking use of language when you read a poem and be able to discuss the associations of certain words.

heat · energy · comfort · rage · FIRE · destruction · temper · life · burning

Tasks

1. Using your dictionary, look up the denotation (literal meaning) of the following words:
   (a) alien (b) water (c) life (d) disgusting (e) amazing (f) heroic (g) fight.
2. In groups, make lists of connotations (associations) of each of the words, as in the example of 'fire' above.

2. Sound

You should be aware of the impact of **sound techniques.** The sound of a poem, its '*verbal music*', can often indicate its main theme or purpose. Poems are best read aloud. In the examination, read the poem aloud in your head and identify any techniques which add to the quality of the poem. The following (a) – (e) are some of the most common sound techniques used in poems.

Unit 2: Poetry

(a) Alliteration

This is where **words begin with the same letter**, creating a certain type of music and linking ideas e.g. '*I hear Lake water Lapping with Low sounds by the shore*'. The alliteration on the 'l' sound creates a gentle flowing motion in the line. The sound of the lapping lake water is low and gentle. Compare this to '*Over the Cobbles he Clattered and Clashed*', where the alliteration on a hard 'c' consonant imitates the harsh noise made by a horse's hooves on an uneven surface. Watch out for alliteration in all your studied poems and also in any unseen poems. Be ready to comment on its effect. It is not just enough to say it is there!

(b) Assonance

This refers to the **patterns made by vowel sounds**. The main vowels are 'a', 'e', 'i', 'o' and 'u', but 'w' and 'y' can also sometimes act as vowel sounds. Vowels can be long or short. Compare the 'a' sound in the word '**cage**' with the 'a' sound in the word '**cat**'. **Long vowels slow down the pace** of a poem and can be used to show sadness or grief:

> '*Alone, alone, all, all alone, / Alone on a wide wide sea!*'

However, if a poet wants a lively, brisk pace, he or she will use assonance on **short vowels:**

> '*. . . the tedding and the spreading / Of the straw for a bedding*'.

Remember that the same letter can make different sounds. Focus on the sound only, not the letter, when discussing assonance.

Tasks

T

Underline every example of alliteration and circle the assonance in the following verse from '*The Lake Isle of Innisfree*' by W.B. Yeats:

I will arise and go now, and go to Innisfree,
And a small cabin build there, of clay and wattles made:
Nine bean-rows will I have there, a hive for the honey-bee;
And live alone in the bee-loud glade.

(c) Onomatopoeia

This is where a word imitates a sound. e.g. the **buzzing** of the bees, the **puck** of a ball, **the ting, tong, tang** of the guitar, **cuckoo**, **splash**, **crack** etc. Onomatopoeia can add tremendous colour and music to the sound quality of a poem.

Tasks

In pairs, suggest words which imitate the following sounds:

1. A breaking window.
2. Wind blowing though trees.
3. Loud crying.
4. Message alerts on mobile phones.

(d) Rhyme

Rhyme refers to words which sound almost the same: **hair, lair, spare, dare**. Rhyme helps to **emphasise words and make them memorable**. It also **adds to the music** of a poem. Rhymes can appear anywhere in a poem. When the last words of lines rhyme, we call this **end-line rhyme**. This is the most usual type of rhyme; however, a rhyme could also occur within a line or in the middle of a line, where it is referred to as **internal rhyme** or **mid-line rhyme**. The **pattern of rhymes** in a poem is known as its **rhyming scheme**. You can work out the rhyming scheme by giving the last word in each line a letter of the alphabet. Use lower case letters. The following example from *Daffodils* by William Wordsworth shows you how to do this:

I wandered lonely as a cloud (a)
That floats on high o'er vales and hills, (b)
When all at once I saw a crowd, (a)
A host, of golden daffodils; (b)
Beside the lake, beneath the trees, (c)
Fluttering and dancing in the breeze. (c)

A poem does not have to rhyme to be a good poem, but be aware of the contribution rhyme can make to the sound of a poem and its skilful craftsmanship. Also look out for rhymes which occur within lines rather than only at the end of lines. This is called **internal rhyme**.

Tasks

Identify every example of rhyme in the following extract from *Annabel Lee* by Edgar Allan Poe:

For the moon never beams without bringing me dreams
Of the beautiful Annabel Lee;
And the stars never rise but I feel the bright eyes
Of the beautiful Annabel Lee;
And so, all the night-tide, I lie down by the side
Of my darling, my darling, my life and my bride …

(e) Rhythm

Rhythm comes from a Greek word which means **measured motion** and is the pattern of stresses or beats within a line of verse. All speech has a rhythm formed by stressed and unstressed syllables.

A word with only one syllable is called a **monosyllable.**

Rhythm is a natural effect within poetry. Each word has its own rhythm, but a phrase or sentence can have a distinct rhythm too.

Examples:

And the cheers and the jeers of the young muleteers =

dadaDUM, dadaDUM, dadaDUM, dadaDUM.

Humpty Dumpty sat on a wall =

DUM da, DUM da, DUM da da DUM.

Poem and Sample Exam Questions (1)

The poem 'Tarantella', by Hilaire Belloc, uses a wide variety of sound and rhythmic techniques.

Tarantella
by Hilaire Belloc

Do you remember an Inn,
Miranda?
Do you remember an Inn?
And the tedding and the spreading
Of the straw for a bedding,
And the fleas that tease in the High Pyrenees,
And the wine that tasted of tar?
And the cheers and the jeers of the young muleteers
(Under the vine of the dark veranda)?
Do you remember an Inn, Miranda,
Do you remember an Inn?
And the cheers and the jeers of the young muleteers
Who hadn't got a penny,
And who weren't paying any,
And the hammer at the doors and the din?
And the hip! hop! hap!
Of the clap
Of the hands to the swirl and the twirl
Of the girl gone chancing,
Glancing,
Dancing,
Backing and advancing,
Snapping of the clapper to the spin
Out and in--
And the ting, tong, tang of the guitar!
Do you remember an Inn,
Miranda?
Do you remember an Inn?

Never more;
Miranda,
Never more.
Only the high peaks hoar*;
And Aragon a torrent at the door.
No sound
In the walls of the halls where falls
The tread
Of the feet of the dead to the ground,
No sound:
But the boom
Of the far waterfall like doom.

hoar = frost

Questions

1. Identify three examples of alliteration used in the poem 'Tarantella' and explain the effect this technique has on the poem. Lay out your answer to this and questions 2-5 in the following format:
    Example:
    Effect: _____
    _____
    _____
    _____

2. From the first verse select three examples of assonance and explain the effect this sound technique has on the poem.

3. Rhyme is used extensively in this poem. Identify three examples of end-line rhyme and three examples of mid-line rhyme.

4. Onomatopoeia is used several times in the poem. Select three examples of onomatopoeia and explain how this affects and adds to the poem.

5. The last verse contrasts sharply with the first verse in this poem. Identify three ways in which the verses are different and explain why you think the poet has created this contrast.

6. **Making Connections:** Choose a poem which you have studied which is remarkable for its sound qualities. Name the poem and the poet. Write three paragraphs in which you identify and discuss the techniques used by the poet in your chosen poem.

3. Subject Matter and Theme

You should be able to comment on subject matter and theme. You need to understand what the poem is about and what is its purpose. For example, 'Dulce et Decorum Est', by Wilfred Owen, is a poem **about** the horrors endured by soldiers during World War I. Dreadful scenes of suffering are described. We call this the **subject matter** of the poem.

However, the poem was written for the **purpose** of showing that it is not a glorious or sweet thing to die in war. This point or message of the poem is called the **theme.** As you can see from this example, **subject matter and theme are very closely connected but are not the same thing.**

Tip:
Remember to ask yourself what the poem is **about** and **why** it was written.

69

The purpose of a poem could be simply to **entertain or amuse** the reader e.g. *'On the Ning Nang Nong'* by Spike Milligan.

On the Ning Nang Nong
Where the Cows go Bong!
and the monkeys all say BOO!

Some poems are written to mock something or somebody. We call this latter type of poem a **satire.** These poems often use **humour, exaggeration, or ridicule** to **criticise** stupidity or evil e.g. *Base Details* by Siegfried Sassoon.

Poem and Sample Exam Questions (2)

Background: The Great Famine, also referred to as 'The Great Hunger', that lasted between 1845 and 1849 was one of the greatest disasters in Irish history. Many starving people tried to gain admission to workhouses which provided them with a small amount of food and clothing in return for hard labour. Unfortunately, diseases related to starvation spread quickly in the overcrowded workhouses and many people were either turned away or left the workhouse to avoid contracting disease.

Quarantine
by Eavan Boland

In the worst hour of the worst season
    of the worst year of a whole people
a man set out from the workhouse with his wife.
He was walking — they were both walking — north.

She was sick with famine fever and could not keep up.
    He lifted her and put her on his back.
He walked like that west and west and north.
Until at nightfall under freezing stars they arrived.

In the morning they were both found dead.
    Of cold. Of hunger. Of the toxins of a whole history.
But her feet were held against his breastbone.
The last heat of his flesh was his last gift to her.

Let no love poem ever come to this threshold.
    There is no place here for the inexact
praise of the easy graces and sensuality of the body.
There is only time for this merciless inventory*:

Their death together in the winter of 1847.
    Also what they suffered. How they lived.
And what there is between a man and woman.
And in which darkness it can best be proved.

Quarantine = a place of isolation for people who may have been exposed to a contagious disease
inventory = an itemised list

Questions

Exploration of Poem

1. State briefly, in 3 or 4 sentences, the subject matter of this poem.
2. What, in your opinion, is the theme of this poem? Explain your response with reference to key lines in the poem.
3. Explain the effect of the repetition of certain words in the first verse of the poem.
4. The poet says that the man and woman died 'of the toxins of a whole history'. What do you think she means by this?
5. In what way does this poem differ from usual poems about love?
6. Read the following medical report which was written in 1847 by a doctor and answer the questions that follow:

Meeting held on the 12th March 1847.

Medical Report

In the fever hospital and infirmary, we have 129 patients in fever and 24 labouring under diarrhoea and other diseases. Out of the 129 now in fever, 5 are new cases taken into hospital today.

We have had 22 deaths since Friday of which a good many were taken into the house on that day and previous.

In fact, the people are coming into the house for the sake of getting coffins. One woman named ………… aged 60 died in 2 hours after the master took her in off the side of the road. I need not inform the guardians of the state of destitution in which most of the paupers are taken in. A great number of them are all but dead and are in such a state from bowel complaints that it is almost impossible to go near them. Their constitutions are so broken down that medical treatment is of little or no use.

Charles Finucane.
M.R.C.S.L.

(i)   What is the subject matter of this report?

(ii) How would you describe the style of writing in this report?

(iii) What is the main difference between a report such as this and the poem 'Quarantine' by Eavan Boland? Explain your response.

(iv) Which of these texts makes the stronger impact on you? Explain your answer by reference to both texts.

7. Examine these two images which are connected to the Great Irish Famine. Which of these two images, in your view, captures the suffering of the Great famine best? You may like to consider aspects such as use of colour, light, background, posture and facial expressions of subjects etc. in your response.

8. **Making Connections**

    'The more familiar you become with a poem, the deeper your understanding of that poem becomes.'

    Select a poem you have studied and explain how this statement applies to your understanding of this poem. Use the poem to support your ideas.

Poem and Sample Exam Questions (3)

Read the poem 'Interruption to a Journey' by Norman MacCaig and answer the questions which follow.

Interruption to a Journey

By Norman MacCaig

The hare we had run over
Bounced about the road
On the springing curve
Of its spine.

Cornfields breathed in the darkness,
We were going through the darkness and
The breathing cornfields from one
Important place to another.

We broke the hare's neck
And made that place, for a moment,
The most important place there was,
Where a bowstring was cut
And a bow broken forever
That had shot itself through so many
Darknesses and cornfields.

It was left in that landscape.
It left us in another.

Questions

?

Exploration of Poem

1. The poet says that he and another person or people were going '…*from one / Important place to another*', and later describes the place where the hare was killed as '*The most important place there was*'. What do you think he means by these statements in the context of this poem?

2. Which of the following statements best describes the theme of this poem? Explain your choice, or, suggest a different sentence to sum up the theme.
    A. Drivers need to be very careful when driving through the dark.
    B. The people in the vehicle did not care very much about the death of the hare.
    C. The journey of life, for all living beings, can be suddenly interrupted by death.

3. The poet says that, '*Cornfields breathed in the darkness*' and refers again to '*The breathing cornfields*'. What do you think he means and how do these words link to the theme of the poem?

4. Select an example of alliteration from the poem and comment on its effect in the poem.

5. **Making Connections**

    Select a poem which you have studied which deals with the subject of death. Name the poet and give the title of the poem. What point or message about death is conveyed in the poem? In your response you should comment on how language and imagery are connected to the theme.

6. **Letter Writing**

    Your dog has been killed on the road. Write a letter to a friend explaining what happened and how you felt about the loss of your pet.

4. Tone

The tone of a poem refers to the **atmosphere** created in the poem and the **feelings** of both the poet (or an imagined speaker) and the reader. Think of **tone of voice** and how it changes if someone is happy or sad, angry or calm, bitter or pleased about something. Poems are ideally meant to be read aloud, which helps establish tone. However, the **words chosen** and the **images** used in a poem can convey powerful feelings and create atmosphere. Ask yourself the following questions: What is **the atmosphere** or **mood** of this poem? How is it created? What is **the poet feeling** about his subject matter? **What do I feel** after reading the poem? Make sure that you can **explain** the answers to these questions and **find evidence** to back up your points.

Poem and Sample Exam Questions (4)

Base Details

By Siegfried Sassoon

If I were fierce, and bald, and short of breath
I'd live with scarlet Majors at the Base,
And speed glum heroes up the line to death.
You'd see me with my puffy petulant face,
Guzzling and gulping in the best hotel,
Reading the Roll of Honour. "Poor young chap,"
I'd say — "I used to know his father well;
Yes, we've lost heavily in this last scrap."
And when the war is done and youth stone dead,
I'd toddle safely home and die — in bed.

Responding to the Poem

1. Siegfried Sassoon fought in World War I and was extremely critical of those who commanded operations. What evidence is there in the above poem to show the poet's attitude to war? Explain your response.

2. Select three examples of alliteration from the poem and, in the case of each, explain the effect of alliteration on the tone of the poem.

3. The poet uses contrast very effectively in this poem. Identify two examples of contrast and show how each contributes to the theme of the poem.

4. Using letters (a,b,c,d etc.), write out the rhyming scheme of this poem. Comment on the use of the rhyming couplet at the end of the poem, explaining its effect on the reader.

5. *'If I were fierce, and bald, and short of breath*
   I'd live with scarlet Majors at the Base,
   And speed glum heroes up the line to death.'
   Which of the following words best describes the poet's tone in these lines? Explain your answer.   A. Sincere   B. Satirical   C. Angry   D. Sad

6. **Making Connections**
   Choose a poem which you have studied which creates a strong atmosphere or mood. Explain how the poet created the mood. You may like to refer to word choice, imagery, rhyme, rhythm, sound techniques, etc.

5. Point of view

You should be able to identify the speaker or voice in the poem.
Poets do not always write from their own point of view. They often adopt **a *persona*** (a role or character) to express an **attitude.** When you read a poem, ask yourself if the 'I' in the poem is really the poet speaking personally or if it is a persona, adopted to mimic somebody or mock an idea. **Show how you know that it is not the poet speaking in his or her own voice but in that of a created persona.**
For example, in the poem *'Base Details',* by Siegfried Sassoon, the poet creates a character to make a point about double standards. The poet himself is not the speaker in the poem.

6. Imagery

You need to be able to comment on the use of imagery. **Imagery** refers to the **pictures which can be formed in the imagination** as one reads a poem. Poets usually strive to make their images original in order to convey their meaning. Most images relate to **familiar** things, so that the reader can draw on their own experience or memory and make the necessary connections.

Always look for images or words which involve the senses and make you see, hear, touch, taste or smell; these **sensuous images** create a very powerful impact on the reader.

A **simile** is a stated likeness of one thing to another, using **'like'** or **'as'**. In *'Dulce et Decorum Est'*, Wilfred Owen uses powerful similes to describe the plight of the weary soldiers. He describes them as being *'like old beggars under sacks... coughing like hags'*. These similes are **based on familiar things,** so we can visualise the men, but the images are **original and striking** because we do not expect this depiction of heroic men fighting a war as being like old beggars hauling sacks.

A **metaphor** compares two things **without using 'like' or 'as'**. For example, we could describe a man as being **'like a lion in battle'** (simile) or we could say that **'he was a lion in battle'** (metaphor). The metaphor makes a stronger impact here, as it suggests that the man almost became a lion in his strength and ferocity.

A **symbol** is an image which represents or stands for something else. For example, a dove is often used as a symbol for peace.

Personification is a figure of speech in which a thing, an idea or an animal is given human characteristics. The non-human objects are portrayed in such a way that we feel they have the ability to act like human beings. For example, in Emily Dickinson's poem *'Because I could not stop for Death'*, death is personified as a person who politely stops a carriage to collect somebody and then brings them to 'Immortality':

> *'Because I could not stop for Death,*
> *He kindly stopped for me;*
> *The carriage held but just ourselves*
> *And Immortality.'*

Similes, metaphors, symbols and personification are not just used for decoration in a poem. They have a very important function in helping the reader to experience and look more deeply into the poem.

When you are discussing images say **why they are appropriate** and **how effective** they are in communicating the theme and tone of the poem.

In the poem *'Nettles'* by Vernon Scannell, the nettles symbolise all those things in life which can cause a person pain.

Poem and Sample Exam Questions (5)

Nettles

By Vernon Scannell

My son aged three fell in the nettle bed.
'Bed' seemed a curious name for those green spears,
That regiment of spite behind the shed:
It was no place for rest. With sobs and tears
The boy came seeking comfort and I saw
White blisters beaded on his tender skin.
We soothed him till his pain was not so raw.
At last he offered us a watery grin,
And then I took my billhook, honed the blade
And went outside and slashed in fury with it
Till not a nettle in that fierce parade
Stood upright any more. And then I lit
A funeral pyre* to burn the fallen dead,
But in two weeks the busy sun and rain
Had called up tall recruits behind the shed:
My son would often feel sharp wounds again.

pyre = a fire for burning a corpse.

Questions

1. Select three examples of personification from the poem 'Nettles' and in each case explain why they are examples of personification rather than metaphors.

2. The poet ends the poem by saying, '*My son would often feel sharp wounds again*'. Which of the following options best explains what the poet meant? Explain your choice.

   A. His son would probably fall into the nettle bed again.

   B. He cannot protect his son from the suffering which life brings.

   C. Nettles are almost impossible to eliminate from a garden.

3. Vernon Scannell fought in World War Two. What images from the poem are connected to his experience as a soldier fighting an enemy? Comment on each image you select, paying careful attention to word choice.

4. The word '**enjambment**' (also spelled 'enjambement') refers to the continuation of one line of verse into the next line without a pause. This creates flow and sometimes gives a sense of urgency or overflowing emotion to the poem. These lines are often referred to as 'run-on lines' because they seem to run over the end of the line into the next.

   Identify an example of **enjambment** in this poem and comment on why you think the poet uses it.

Making Connections

5. Compare the theme of '*Nettles*' by Vernon Scannell to the theme of '*Praise Song for My Mother*', by Grace Nichols on page 79.

6. What are the differences in punctuation, rhyme, rhythm and structure in '*Nettles*' and '*Praise Song for My Mother*'?

7. Which poem do you prefer and why?

Praise Song for My Mother

By Grace Nichols

You were
water to me
deep and bold and fathoming

You were
moon's eye to me
pull and grained and mantling

You were
sunrise to me
rise and warm and streaming

You were
the fishes red gill to me
the flame tree's spread to me
the crab's leg/the fried plantain* smell
               replenishing replenishing

Go to your wide futures, you said

plantain = a kind of banana which grows
in the tropics and is usually cooked by frying

B. Answering Exam Questions on Unseen Poetry

1. Step-by-Step Approach
The following steps are a guide to answering exam questions on unseen poetry.

Step One

■ **Read the questions** you are required to answer on the unseen poem. **Highlight** the important words in each question and make sure that you do not leave out any part of the questions.

■ **Read the poem carefully**. This will give you a general idea of its subject matter. Do not worry if you do not understand every word or line of the poem.

Step Two

■ Beginning with the first question, **read over the poem again marking off any words or phrases** which you think will be useful as support for your response. **Keep asking yourself questions**.

For example, if you are asked what impression you got of a person or scene, ask yourself **why** you got that impression, what **words** created it, **why** did the poet pick certain words, etc. This will help to give your response a sharp focus.

Step Three

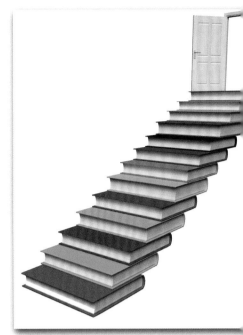

- **Write your answer**. Answers may be very short or more developed, depending on the question and the marks given. They **must always be relevant** to the question asked. If you find yourself paraphrasing or telling the story of the poem, STOP! You are probably moving away from the question. Check again to see what the question asked you to do. Now continue your answer, keeping an eye on **exactly what you have been asked.**

- Make sure that you **support your points** with quotation from, or reference to the poem. There is no need to write out chunks of the poem. This will not get you marks and is a waste of precious time. **Choose quotations carefully.** It may be that one word or a short phrase will illustrate the point you are making.

- Try to **respond personally**. You will be rewarded for showing that you understand what the poet is saying and that you can connect to the poem. Ask yourself how the poem made you **feel**. Why did you feel like that? Then ask yourself if there is anything in the poem that is **relevant to your life**. What is it? How is it relevant? **Is there anything you learnt from the poem?**

2. Exam Focus

In the exam, you may be specifically asked to:

- **Respond to Language:** Look carefully at the poet's **use of language**. Are there any words or phrases that you thought were particularly effective or clever? Ask yourself why you thought this.

- **Respond to Imagery**: Examine the poem carefully, checking for any use of **simile** or **metaphor**. If you can identify a good image, comment on its effectiveness. Say why you thought it was a good image and how it contributes to the poem's message.

- **Respond to Sound**: Examine the poet's use of sound. Does the poem rhyme? Is there any use of alliteration, assonance or onomatopoeia?

- **Say whether you liked or did not like the poem.** You must explain your answer here. It is not enough to just state that you did or didn't like the poem. When answering, you should consider all of the KEY SKILLS for responding to a poem which are listed on page 64.

Tip:
Take care with spelling and punctuation, especially when you quote from the poem. Conclude each answer with a reference back to the question asked.

Sample Questions and Answers on Unseen Poem (1)

Mrs. Reece Laughs

By Martin Armstrong

Laughter, with us, is no great undertaking,
A sudden wave that breaks and dies in breaking.
Laughter with Mrs. Reece is much less simple:
It germinates, it spreads, dimple by dimple,
From small beginnings, things of easy girth,
To formidable redundancies of mirth.
Clusters of subterranean chuckles rise
And presently the circles of her eyes
Close into slits and all the woman heaves
As a great elm with all its mounds of leaves
Wallows before the storm. From hidden sources
A mustering of blind volcanic forces
Takes her and shakes her till she sobs and gapes.
Then all that load of bottled mirth escapes
In one wild crow, a lifting of huge hands,
And creaking stays, a visage that expands
In scarlet ridge and furrow. Thence collapse,
A hanging head, a feeble hand that flaps
An apron-end to stir an air and waft
A steaming face. And Mrs. Reece has laughed.

Questions

?

1. What impression of Mrs. Reece do you form from reading this poem? Support your answer with reference to the poem.
2. How does the poet, Martin Armstrong, capture the extraordinary nature of Mrs. Reece's laughter in this poem? Explain your answer with reference to the poem.

Sample Answers to Unseen Poem

1. From reading this poem, I have formed the impression that Mrs. Reece is a very large woman, good-humoured and possessing an almost overwhelming personality.

   The poet describes her as being like a 'great elm with all its mounds of leaves'. Phrases like 'volcanic forces', 'huge hands' and 'creaking stays' all contribute to the impression that she is a very large woman.

   She certainly has a great sense of humour which expresses itself in this wonderful laughter. It 'Takes her and shakes her till she sobs and gapes'. This description conveys the strong impression that she is a woman who can see the fun in situations. Her laughter is 'bottled' up until it explodes in 'redundancies of mirth'.

   I think Mrs. Reece could be an overwhelming personality. She does not seem to be able to control her laughter and it could be quite intimidating, although funny, when she lets out 'one wild crow' that turns her face 'scarlet.' I can just imagine how she might react if something made her angry!

   In general, I get the impression that Mrs. Reece is a larger-than-life character in every sense of the word.

2. Martin Armstrong captures the extraordinary nature of Mrs. Reece's laughter by using very graphic, detailed imagery.

   A series of images appeals to our senses of sight and hearing. We are able to see her smile spreading 'dimple by dimple', her eyes closing into 'slits' and her whole body heaving with laughter. We can hear the 'chuckles' the 'sobs' and the 'loud crow' as the laughter escapes. By using such sensuous details in the description, the poet makes the readers feel as though they have actually witnessed the extraordinary event themselves.

   Armstrong also uses splendid metaphors and similes, drawn from nature, to bring out the dramatic quality of the laughter. 'Clusters of subterranean chuckles rise' to the surface and she 'heaves / As a great elm with all its mound of leaves'. The reference to a 'storm' and 'blind volcanic forces' are very powerful in capturing the extraordinary, powerful nature of her laughter.

   By describing the draining effect which the laughter has had on Mrs Reece, Armstrong captures the exhaustion which results from such a unique explosion of mirth. She is left with 'a hanging head' and feebly tries to cool her 'steaming face' with the end of her apron.

   Armstrong certainly succeeded in capturing the unusual laughter of his subject. I found myself laughing as I read, which was quite an extraordinary experience for me!

Sample Questions and Answers on Unseen Poem (2)

Lovers on Aran

By Seamus Heaney

The timeless waves, bright, sifting, broken glass,
Came dazzling around, into the rocks,
Came glinting, sifting from the Americas

To possess Aran.
Or did Aran rush
to throw wide arms of rock around a tide
That yielded with an ebb, with a soft crash?

Did sea define the land or land the sea?
Each drew new meaning from the waves' collision.

Sea broke on land to full identity.

1. Identify a line or phrase in the poem where the poet uses each of the following poetic techniques and explain why you think the poet uses the technique.
   Contrast
   Personification
   Tone
   Assonance
   Enjambment
2. What do you think the message of the poem is? Explain your answer.
3. Evaluate how one of the poetic techniques helps convey the message you have identified in the poem.

Junior Cycle Final Examination 20XX, Sample 3

English – Higher Level

Sample Answers to Unseen Poem

1. **Contrast:** 'Did sea define the land or land the sea?'
    This line uses contrast to highlight the difference in power which exists between the land and the sea. The hardness of the land and the yielding quality of the sea have already been contrasted to show how two completely opposite things can depend on each other to co-exist. The contrast, which is posed as a question, highlights and emphasises difference but subtly suggests a unity.

    Personification: 'throw wide arms of rock around a tide/That yielded'
    The land and waves are presented as 'lovers' as if they are embracing each other. This technique helps us to see natural forces with fresh eyes, as though they were living beings. Both the land and sea become mysterious again, making us ask where does all this energy come from?

    Tone: 'Sea broke on land to full identity'.
    The tone of the poem seems calm, due to the repetition of 'soft' and words like 'dazzling' and 'glinting'. There is almost a sense of awe beneath this calm, as the poet wonders about impossible questions. However, this closing line about 'full identity' captures the tone of quiet triumph.

    Assonance: 'The timeless waves, bright, sifting, broken glass'
    The assonance on the long vowel in 'time' and 'bright' in this line adds to the musical quality of the poem and slows down the pace in keeping with the calm atmosphere.

    Enjambment: 'did Aran rush / to throw wide arms of rock around a tide /That yielded with an ebb, ...'
    The lines flowing into each other capture the flowing movement of the tide coming in, which is cleverly presented as though it is the land actually rushing toward the sea. The flow then breaks with the comma after 'ebb', imitating waves ebbing back suddenly. The rhythm therefore imitates the movement of the sea.

2. I think the poem is exploring the idea that things come to be (or know what they are) only by interacting with what they are not. The foreignness of the waves ('sifting from the Americas') is emphasized here. The poem suggests that whether it is lovers, nations, or physical features of geography, contrast is the key to recognizing what something is. I think it's an open-minded message. Trust in difference and accept it, the poet seems to be saying.

3. The use of personification strikes me most. There is something very intense about two creatures in love. It's also interesting to see how violently the waves bash the west coast of Ireland and look at all that energy and think not of violence but of love. It makes me wonder about the line between passion (as love) and passion as suffering. The closing line is full of wonder at the strangeness of love: 'Sea broke on land to full identity.' Usually we think of identity as being wholly ourselves, and unbroken, but Heaney seems to be saying that full identity is letting go of 'me' and becoming 'us'. I think he is suggesting that people who don't trust enough to love, or travel, or get out of their narrow sense of who and what they are, can never fully know themselves, or anything else.

Sample Questions and Answers on Unseen Poem (3)

Seeing and Believing

By Edwin Romond

The girls giggled
but the boys laughed right out loud
when Mrs. Stone raged crimson
holding my eighth grade project:
"The Map of New Jersey."
"Get up here, boy!"
and I had no choice
but to walk the gangplank to her desk
where my map choked in her fist.
"What's this jazz? Huh?
The ocean is not green, Bub, it's blue.
Ya' get it? Blue, blue, blue, blue!"
punching my map with each word into my chest.
My classmates roared a chorus
of "Green ocean! Green ocean!"
their voices rising in waves of laughter
as I carried the wrinkled and ripped map
back to my seat through their sneers.
Soon, all their maps perimetered the room
leaving me adrift in the memory of a Sunday
when, in the October air,
my father and I walked over seashells
and I, only nine,
remarked that the ocean looked green.
My father, peering out from beneath his cap,
said, "Yes, it does" and his fingers swam
through my hair.

Questions

What aspects of the poem *Seeing and Believing*, would make it suitable for dramatisation? Explain your answer by reference to the poem.   15 marks

Junior Cycle Final Examination 2018

English – Higher Level

Sample Answers to Unseen Poem

In my opinion, this poem would be very suitable for dramatisation due to several key aspects.

The excellent creation of a distinct **setting** gives it instant dramatic appeal. I find it easy to visualise the classroom full of children and the teacher holding the boy's map which was 'choked in her fist'. Walking the 'gangplank' to her desk suggests an old-fashioned classroom where children sat in orderly rows with aisles in between. This setting, with appropriate **props**, could easily be created for a short dramatic scene and I would put the boy at the back of the class so that his dreaded walk to the teacher's desk would be longer and make more impact.

The use of **effective dialogue** and the other **sounds** in the poem also make it very suitable for dramatisation. The voice of the teacher is abrupt and harsh when she orders the speaker to 'Get up here, boy!' and gives an excellent insight into her **character**. The sound of children giggling and laughing in the background creates **contrast** with the teacher's voice which adds to the **dramatic tension** and highlights the embarrassment experienced by the boy.

In addition, there are very clear indications of **physical gestures**. The teacher asks questions: 'What's this jazz? Huh?' while punching the map into the boy's chest repeatedly. The class responds by roaring a 'chorus' of 'Green ocean! Green ocean!' which rises in intensity as the dejected boy returns to his seat, carrying his 'wrinkled and ripped map'. These **actions and reactions** of characters are key components of all drama.

Finally, if this poem were being dramatised for a short film, the shift of scene to the boy walking along the beach with his father would make a superb contrast to the classroom scene and have its own appeal in the gentle dialogue and the loving physical gesture where the father runs his fingers through his son's hair.

For all of the above reasons, I believe this poem would be extremely successful as a short dramatic piece for either stage or film.

Sample Questions and Answers to Poetry

Junior Cycle 20XX Sample 3

1. Imagine you are writing a poem. Outline a message you would like to convey in your poem. The poem could be about something personal, social, universal or a combination of all three.

   I'd like to write a poem called 'Stronghold' about how memories fade over time and yet can leave a deep impression. I have noticed recently that when I try to remember my childhood, I can't see any particular scene very vividly, but I still feel strong nostalgia. For instance, I can recollect going to the beach as a toddler and loving it, but only bits and pieces of detail remain. The rest is lost. I wonder if remembering only impressions makes childhood seem better or worse than it was.

2. Suggest an image you would use in your poem as outlined above and explain why you feel that would be an appropriate image to use.

   I would use an image of a child making a sandcastle. You scoop up the wet sand and fill a plastic mould, and then plonk it down and make a little shape. A castle is a tough place where powerful people keep all their riches, and it should be able to withstand serious assaults. But a child's sandcastle is the weakest thing in the world because anything can destroy it: a wet dog, a Frisbee, anything. Eventually the water will come and wash the imaginary castle away, leaving only a trace behind in the form of a lump. I think my childhood memories are vague, like that lump, but they still contain a kind of treasure: the memory of the pleasure of making something purely for fun.

C. Answering Exam Questions on Studied Poetry

The questions in this section will allow you to show your knowledge of and response to poems which you have studied.

Revise the **Key Skills for Reading and Responding to a Poem** provided on page 64 of this unit.

Make sure that you are clear on the **theme, tone, point of view, imagery, language** and **sound** of each poem studied. You should be able to demonstrate the part played by each of these elements of poetry.

1. Step-by-Step Approach
The following steps are a guide to answering questions on the exam paper on unseen poetry.

Step One
- **Read questions carefully**, underlining the exact task or tasks. Make sure that you do not forget any part of any question. **Highlight** key words.
- Think of the poems you have prepared and select a suitable one to answer on. You may need more than one poem if the question demands it.

Step Two

- **Plan your answer**. Quickly brainstorm relevant points. Think of **suitable quotations** to support these points.
- **Organise your points** into a logical order. Make sure that you are not repeating yourself if there are different parts to the question. Each question will require a different response.

Step Three

- Write your answer. **Name the poem and the poet** at the beginning of your response. You will be given a space to do this on the answer booklet.
- Briefly **introduce your response** using the wording of the question.
- Make approximately THREE relevant points using the **Point, Quotation, Explanation** – PQE method. ONE point per paragraph.
- Briefly **conclude** your response. Refer to the wording in the question as you conclude.

2. Exam Focus

Sample Questions and Answers on Studied Poem

Questions

1. (a) From the poetry you have studied, choose one poem in which the poet uses interesting language to convey powerful thoughts and feelings. Give the poet's name and the title of the poem.

   (b) What powerful thoughts and feelings are conveyed by the poet in your chosen poem? Support your answer with reference to the poem.

   (c) Explain what you find interesting about the language used by the poet in the poem you have chosen. Support your answer with reference to the poem.

Note: The poem 'Dulce et Decorum Est' by Wilfred Owen is being used as an example of a studied poem.

Dulce et Decorum Est

By Wilfred Owen

Bent double, like old beggars under sacks,

Knock-kneed, coughing like hags, we cursed through sludge,

Till on the haunting flares we turned our backs,

And towards our distant rest began to trudge.

Men marched asleep. Many had lost their boots,

But limped on, blood-shod. All went lame, all blind;

Drunk with fatigue; deaf even to the hoots

Of tired, outstripped Five-Nines that dropped behind.

Gas! GAS! Quick, boys! – An ecstasy of fumbling

Fitting the clumsy helmets just in time;

But someone still was yelling out and stumbling

And flound'ring like a man in fire or lime. –

Dim through the misty panes and thick green light,

As under a green sea, I saw him drowning.

In all my dreams before my helpless sight,

He plunges at me, guttering, choking, drowning.

If in some smothering dreams, you too could pace

Behind the wagon that we flung him in,

And watch the white eyes writhing in his face,

His hanging face, like a devil's sick of sin,

If you could hear, at every jolt, the blood

Come gargling from the froth-corrupted lungs

Obscene as cancer, bitter as the cud

Of vile, incurable sores on innocent tongues, –

My friend, you would not tell with such high zest

To children ardent for some desperate glory,

The old Lie: *Dulce et decorum est*

Pro patria mori.

Note: Underlining and PQE (Point, Quotation, Explanation) marks are inserted here for demonstration purposes only. You will not insert these into your response.

Sample Answers to Studied Poem

(a) 'Dulce et Decorum Est' by Wilfred Owen.

(b) I have chosen the poem 'Dulce et Decorum Est' by Wilfred Owen, to demonstrate how a poet can convey powerful thoughts and feelings through the use of interesting language.

The powerful opening of the poem makes one **think** of how war breaks the spirits of soldiers. [P] Instead of the glorious future, promised by war propaganda, they are reduced to the level of a pitiful procession of broken men, more like old 'hags' than heroes. **Feelings** of pity are evoked in the reader as they imagine the suffering, weariness and despair as the soldiers 'cursed through sludge', 'marched asleep' and 'limped' back to their base. **[Q+E]**

Following on from this image, the poet explores the **thought** that no soldier, who has experienced the horror of seeing others die, ever really escapes from the memory. [P] The poet cannot forget that he saw a comrade 'flound'ring like a man in fire or lime', 'drowning 'in the 'green sea' of a gas attack. **Feelings** of the same **helplessness** which he experienced at the time, come back to haunt him. The **fear**, as the soldier 'plunges' at him, 'guttering' and 'choking' never leaves his memory. [Q+E]

The powerful ending of the poem presents the major **theme or thought** to the readers.[P] The poet is **disgusted** by the 'old Lie', which is told with 'high zest' to innocent school children. He declares that it is neither noble nor sweet to die for your country on the battlefield. The poem ends on this note of **anger and disgust** for the masking of truth. **[Q+E]**

(c) This poem, powerful in both thoughts and feelings, had a strong impact on me. I thought that the poet used extremely interesting language techniques in this poem. **Superb images** are employed to graphically describe the procession of weary men. [P] Owen compares them to 'old beggars under sacks' and 'hags'. These **images are interesting** because create a stark **contrast** to the expectations of 'glory', which the soldiers once cherished. The **language** chosen **emphasises their degradation** in war. **[Q+E]**

The **use of verbs** such as 'coughing', 'cursed', 'began to trudge', all conjure up the atmosphere of despair and fatigue. [P] The **pace** of the poem is slow and tedious. **Sentences are varied in length** and broken up by **punctuation** marks. This gives the impression of the uneven steps taken by men who are 'drunk with fatigue'. The **sudden change of pace**, as the gas attack occurs is also reflected in the **skilful**

and interesting choice of verbs – 'fumbling', 'yelling out', 'stumbling', 'floundering'. This **use of contrast** powerfully creates the panic and horror and leaves a permanent impression on the mind of the reader. **[Q+E]**

The most interesting example of dramatic use of language occurs in the description of the gas attack. **[P]**. The panic of the men is captured in the imperative 'Gas! GAS! Quick, boys!' . The use of the word 'ecstasy' to describe the 'fumbling' to fit the masks in time is both interesting and terrifying. We don't usually associate ecstasy with such horror. The language engages the senses in a powerful way. We see the unfortunate man's 'hanging face, like a devil's sick of sin'. We hear his howls of pain and the 'gargling' of blood in his throat as he chokes to death. We almost feel the jolting of the wagon and the violence of his body being 'flung' into it. **[Q+E]**

The use of language throughout this poem is not only interesting, it is memorable and disturbing. It forces us to confront the reality that war is far from being sweet and honourable.

Checklist

Use the following checklist to ensure that you have complied with the demands of the marking scheme:

1. Have I practised writing both unseen and studied poetry responses? ☐

2. Have I prepared at least 15-20 poems following the guidelines for analysing poems? ☐

3. Have I read the questions very carefully and ensured that I am addressing all parts of the questions? ☐

4. Have I underlined the key words in all questions before answering? ☐

5. Have I made a short plan, ensuring that I am addressing the question? ☐

6. Have I made relevant points and supported them with quotation from the poem/s? ☐

7. Have I offered some explanation of my points? ☐

8. Have I shown my personal reactions to the poem in the course of my answer? ☐

9. Have I paragraphed properly, developing one point in each paragraph? ☐

10. Have I checked my spelling, punctuation and grammar? ☐

    If you can tick each of these boxes, you will be able to answer questions on both unseen and studied poetry.

03 Fiction

Learning Outcomes

This unit addresses the following learning outcomes:
OL8, R1, 2, 3, 4, 6, 7, 8, 9; W1, 3, 7, 8, 9.

In your Final Assessment Examination, you may be required to answer questions on Unseen Fiction and Studied Fiction.

The marks for each question will be clearly indicated on the paper and the space provided for your answer will give you an indication of how much you should write.

Guidance will be given to help you with your time-management and you should pay careful attention to time-limits in order to finish the entire paper within two hours.

In order to do well in this area of the course, you need to have read a wide variety of short stories and novels and to have studied two novels and a selection of short stories in depth.

You will need to use an appropriate critical vocabulary while responding to texts.

Key Skills for Answering on Fiction:

When you respond to fiction texts, you must display an ability to understand and interpret what you read. You are expected in your response to make relevant points, which you can support with reference to the text.

You need to understand each of the following key areas:

Characters	Plot
Setting	Theme

A. Characters

1. Creating Characters

Characters must be credible and interesting in order to engage the reader. Remember that characters are not real people in fiction. They have been created by the writer. Your task is to explain how this is done. Pay very careful attention to the author's word choice in descriptions.

Writers use different methods when creating fictitious characters:

● The reader can be given **direct information** about the character, e.g. 'Mrs O'Connor was a mean-minded, irritable woman, who revelled in causing trouble for the children of the neighbourhood'. Here, we are told what we should think of Mrs O'Connor. There is no room for any doubt, due to the use of specific adjectives 'mean-minded', 'irritable' and the use of the verb 'revelled'.

● **Implied information** can be given through the character's actions. In this case, the writer does not tell us directly, but allows us to form our own opinion of a character based on how they act and/or react in situations. This is the most reliable indication of what a character is like. Look at the following description from *Great Expectations* by Charles Dickens. The characters of both Estella (the girl) and Pip (the child) are suggested to the reader, rather than directly described:

> She came back, with some bread and meat and a little mug of beer. She put the mug down on the stones of the yard, and gave me the bread and meat <u>without looking at me</u>, as <u>insolently</u> as if <u>I were a dog in disgrace</u>. <u>I was so humiliated, hurt, spurned, offended, angry, sorry</u> – <u>I cannot hit upon the right name for the smart</u> – God knows what its name was – <u>that tears started to my eyes</u>. The moment they sprang there, the girl <u>looked at me with a quick delight in having been the cause of them</u>. This gave me <u>power to keep them back</u> and to look at her: so, she gave a <u>contemptuous toss</u> – but with a sense, I thought, of having <u>made too sure that I was so wounded</u> – and left me.

The words and phrases underlined suggest that Estella is a cruel and haughty individual, who enjoys humiliating another child. Pip's reaction to this treatment shows his sensitivity and passionate nature. Although he is deeply offended by Estella's actions and attitude, he maintains his dignity by refusing to cry and by looking straight at his tormentor.

● Many descriptions use a **combination of direct and implied information** to bring the character alive on the page and to stimulate the interest of the reader. We want to know more about them because they intrigue us.

Tasks

1. In each of the following character descriptions identify examples of direct and implied information and comment on the effectiveness of the writer's use of language.

    (a) He was a big, beefy man with hardly any neck, although he did have a very large moustache. Mrs Dursley was thin and blonde and had nearly twice the usual amount of neck, which came in very useful as she spent so much of her time craning over garden fences, spying on the neighbours. (Extract from *Harry Potter and the Philosopher's Stone* by J.K. Rowling.)

    (b) Her skin was a rich black that would have peeled like a plum if snagged, but then no one would have thought of getting close enough to Mrs Flowers to ruffle her dress, let alone snag her skin. (Extract from *I Know Why the Caged Bird Sings* by Maya Angelou.)

(c) Lord Asriel was a tall man with powerful shoulders, a fierce dark face, and eyes that seemed to flash and glitter with savage laughter. It was a face to be dominated by, or to fight; never a face to patronise or pity. (Extract from *Northern Lights* by Philip Pullman.)

2. Imagine that you are writing a novel. Write a short description of each of the characters pictured below, using direct and implied information.

2. Dialogue

What characters say, and the way that they say it, can reveal their attitudes and certain aspects of their personalities. Take, for example, this piece of dialogue from the novel *To Kill a Mockingbird* by Harper Lee. Atticus Finch is speaking to his young daughter, Scout:

> 'First of all', he said, 'if you can learn a simple trick, Scout, you'll get along better with all kinds of folks. You never really understand a person until you consider things from his point of view . . . until you climb into his skin and walk around in it'.

This short excerpt from the dialogue is very revealing. It shows us his attitude to other people and how he is both just and wise. He speaks to Scout in language which she can understand and uses a simple image of walking around in another person's skin to illustrate how to understand other people.

We can also learn about characters from **what others say about them** and from how they relate to other characters. Ask yourself if characters are liked by others and try to explain the reasons why or why not. Are they sincere, friendly, open, cunning, nasty, devious, etc?

What characters say about themselves and their feelings can give us an insight into their personalities, attitudes and motives.

3. Questions on Character

When discussing character, highlight or underline anything which you can use to support your points. Then, jot down a few words to describe the character. Remember that you are looking at qualities or traits of the character – keep that as the central focus. Don't just summarise.

The following pages contain examples of extracts and questions to explore character. Extracts 1–3 are written from the perspective of an individual who is a part of the narrative. We call this **first-person narration**. It is easily recognisable by the use of the pronoun 'I'. When a story is written from the point of view of the narrator, the information the reader gets is based only on the narrator's viewpoint. The reader's understanding of other characters, conflict and plot development are based on what we learn from the narrator.

While this has some limitations, there are also major advantages to the first person point of view. The reader experiences being inside the mind of the narrator, which creates a direct link between them. As the narrator reveals emotions and thoughts to the reader, a personal intimacy is created. It is almost as if the reader is a best friend in whom one can confide. A lot of fiction for young adults use the first person for this exact reason; it creates an immediate connection with the reader.

Extracts 4 and 5 are written from the **third-person** point of view. When writing fiction, **third-person narration** uses 'he', 'she', 'they', 'them', 'his', 'hers' etc.

Extract 1.

Read the edited extract from the novel *Slam* by Nick Hornby and then answer the questions that follow.

Background information

In this edited extract, from the opening of the book, we are introduced to Sam, a skateboard-loving teenager. Sam tells us about himself in his own words. He reveals that he holds imaginary conversations with his skateboarding hero, Tony Hawk.

If I'm going to tell this story properly, without trying to hide anything, then there's something I should own up to, because it's important. Here's the thing. I know it sounds stupid, and I'm not this sort of person usually, honest. I mean, I don't believe in, you know, ghosts or reincarnation or any weird stuff at all. Anyway. I'll just say it and you can think what you want. I talk to Tony Hawk, and Tony Hawk talks back.

Some of you probably won't have heard of Tony Hawk. Well, I'll tell you, but I'll have to say that you should know already. Not knowing Tony Hawk is like not knowing Robbie Williams, or maybe even Tony Blair. It's worse than that, if you think about it, because there are loads of politicians and loads of singers. But there is only one skater, really, and his name's Tony Hawk. Well, there is not only one. But he's definitely the Big One. He's the J.K. Rowling of

skaters, the Big Mac, the iPod, the Xbox. The only excuse I'll accept for not knowing Tony Hawk is that you're not interested in skating.

When I got into skating, my mum bought me a Tony Hawk poster off the Internet. It's the coolest present I've ever had, and it wasn't even the most expensive. And it went straight up onto my bedroom wall, and I just got into the habit of telling it things. At first I only told Tony about skating – I would talk about the problems I was having or the tricks I'd pulled off. I pretty much ran to my room to tell him about the first rock'n'roll* I'd managed, because I knew it would mean much more to a picture of Tony Hawk than it would to a real-life mum. I'm not dissing* my mum, but she hasn't got a clue, really. So when I told her about things like that, she'd try to look all enthusiastic, but there was nothing really going on in her eyes. She was all, 'Oh, that's great'. But if I'd asked her what a rock'n'roll was, she wouldn't have been able to tell me. So what was the point? Tony knew, though. Maybe that was why my mum bought me the poster, so that I'd have someone else to talk to.

rock'n'roll = skateboarding term
dissing = disrespecting

Questions

1. Which of the following sentences best describes Sam's relationship with his mother? Explain your choice using support from the extract.
   (a) They have no understanding of each other.
   (b) Sam loves and respects his mother.
   (c) Sam and his mother love and care about each other although they have different interests.
   (d) Sam finds his mother annoying and clueless.
2. From your reading of the passage, what do you learn about the character of Sam? Support your answer with reference to the extract.
3. What do you think Sam means when he says, 'He's the J.K. Rowling of skaters, the Big Mac, the iPod, the Xbox'?
4. In the extract Sam tells us that he sometimes holds imaginary conversations with his skateboarding hero, Tony Hawk. Based on information from the extract, write out the conversation that might take place between Sam and Tony.
5. From a novel you have read, select a character whom you found particularly unusual or interesting. Write three paragraphs about this character, commenting on the role played by the author's use of description and dialogue. You must name the novel and the author.

Extract 2.

The following extract is taken from the novel *Wonder* by R.J. Palacio. Read the extract and answer the questions that follow.

Background information

The story is narrated by August, a ten-year-old boy born with a terrible facial abnormality, who longs to be accepted as an ordinary child.

I know I'm not an ordinary ten-year-old kid. I mean, sure, I do ordinary things. I eat ice cream. I ride my bike. I play ball. I have an Xbox. Stuff like that makes me ordinary. I guess. And I feel ordinary. Inside. But I know ordinary kids don't make other ordinary kids run away screaming in playgrounds. I know ordinary kids don't get stared at wherever they go.

If I found a magic lamp and I could have one wish, I would wish that I had a normal face that no one ever noticed at all. I would wish that I could walk down the street without people seeing me and then doing that look-away thing. Here's what I think: the only reason I'm not ordinary is that no one else sees me that way.

But I'm kind of used to how I look by now. I know how to pretend I don't see the faces people make. We've all gotten pretty good at that sort of thing: me, Mom and Dad, Via. Actually, I take that back: Via's not so good at it. She can get really annoyed when people do something rude. Like, for instance, one time in the playground some older kids made some noises. I don't even know what the noises were exactly because I didn't hear them myself, but Via heard and she just started yelling at the kids. That's the way she is. I'm not that way.

Via doesn't see me as ordinary. She says she does, but if I were ordinary, she wouldn't feel like she needs to protect me as much. And Mom and Dad don't see me as ordinary, either. They see me as extraordinary. I think the only person in the world who realises how ordinary I am is me.

My name is August, by the way. I won't describe what I look like. Whatever you're thinking, it's probably worse.

Questions

1. Both Sam (extract 1) and August (extract 2) are unusual characters. Name one way in which they are similar to one another, and one way in which they are different.

2. Both Sam and August tell their stories directly to the reader, using the first person pronoun 'I'. How does this affect the way you respond to the characters? Explain your response.

3. What do you think August means when he says: 'the only reason I'm not ordinary is that no one else sees me that way.'?

4. Based on the extract, what do you consider to be the strongest aspects of August's character? Explain your response.

5. From a novel you have studied, select a character who had to overcome some obstacle or deal with a personal problem. Briefly describe the obstacle or problem and comment on the attitude of the character to his/her situation and how he/she felt about it. You must name the novel and the author.

Extract 3.

Read the following extract, adapted from the short story *No Place Like* by Gene Kemp, and answer the questions which follow.

Background information

In this extract, Pete, an accident-prone 16-year-old, discovers that he has forgotten about the toast which he had placed under the grill.

I must have fallen asleep for I came to suddenly woken by the sound not of the universe but loud banging and roaring going on somewhere. I heaved myself off the bed in time to see Dad filling the doorway. Speaking.

'I come home early,' he was saying in a voice loud even for him, 'having spent my lunchtime beavering away on your behalf . . .'

'You needn't have bothered . . .' I began and then sniffed the air. 'Dad, what's that terrible smell?'

My father did a dance up and down in the doorway. For a big man he's light on his feet.

'Aha, so you noticed, did you? You're quick, I'll say that for you. In fact you amaze me. I never fail to be amazed at you through life, but today you have surpassed even yourself "What's that smell?" you ask, standing there like a great goop. That smell, my boy, is the smell of the house burning'.

'The house burning?'

'You heard me. That's what I said. And you understood did you? Clever boy.'

I managed to peer past him to a blue and smoke-filled landing. A strong pong of grilled grill was floating up the stairs.

'Hadn't we better do something?' I tried to push past him.

'Don't worry,' he said soothingly. 'It's all under control. But only because', his voice started to get louder until it beat into my skull like hammer blows, 'I arrived home early full of peace and goodwill towards men, to find what? What indeed?' he bellowed, lowering his face close to mine. 'You might well ask. Half a dozen people crowding round the front door, its bell out of action, telephone engineers trampling all over the garden because the line's been reported out of order, and a fire engine screeching to a halt outside the house. Didn't you even hear that?'

I shook my head.

'The kitchen full of smoke and about to burst into flames!'

I tried to speak and couldn't.

'But don't worry about it. Don't give it a thought. It was just someone who shall be nameless, had left the grill on with toast under it, or what had been toast in earlier times . . .'

1. What impression of Pete's father do you get from reading this extract? Support your answer with reference to the extract.

2. In your opinion, what kind of character is Pete, based on his reactions to the incident described in the extract? Explain your response.

3. Do you think the author meant this to be a serious or a funny incident? Explain your response.

4. Imagine that you are Pete. Write a diary entry, based on the incident.

5. From a novel or short story which you have studied, select two or more characters who engage in conflict (serious or funny) with each other. Explain how the conflict arose, how it developed and how it concluded. Pay particular attention to the role played by the writer's use of dialogue. You must give the title of the novel or short story and name the author.

Extract 4.

Read the following extract from *A Game of Thrones* by George R.R. Martin and answer the questions which follow.

Background information

Here, the point of view is known as **third person** or **omniscient** (all-knowing) narration because the narrator is 'all-knowing'. He/she has created the characters and plot and can see into the minds and thoughts of different characters, presenting the reader with various angles from which they can view events.

Fifteen years past, when they had ridden forth to win a throne, the Lord of Storm's End had been clean-shaven, clear-eyed, and muscled like a maiden's fantasy. Six and a half feet tall, he towered over lesser men, and when he donned the armour and the great antlered helmet of his house, he became a veritable giant. He'd had a giant's strength too, his weapon of choice a spiked iron war-hammer that Ned could scarcely lift. In those days, the smell of leather and blood had clung to him like perfume.

Now it was perfume that clung to him like perfume, and he had a girth to match his height. Ned had last seen the king nine years before during Balon Greyjoy's rebellion, when the stag and the direwolf* had joined to end the pretensions of the self-proclaimed King of the Iron Islands. Since the night they had stood side by side in Greyjoy's fallen stronghold, where Robert had accepted the rebel lord's surrender and Ned had taken his son Theon as hostage and ward, the king had gained at least eight stone. A beard as coarse and black as iron covered his jaw to hide his double chin and the sag of his royal jowls, but nothing could hide his stomach or the dark circles under his eyes.

direwolf = now extinct species of wolf

1. The writer skilfully shows the changes brought about by time in this description of the Lord of Storm's End. Identify four examples of direct contrast in the extract.

2. Explain the meaning of the following words in the context of the extract:
    (a) Donned
    (b) Veritable
    (c) Girth
    (d) Coarse

3. What is meant by each of these images?
    (a) Muscled like a maiden's fantasy
    (a) Now it was perfume that clung to him like perfume

4. Judging by the above extract, which of the following best describes the genre of *A Game of Thrones*? Give reasons for your response.
    (a) Science fiction
    (b) Fantasy
    (c) Detective story
    (d) Thriller

Extract 5.

This extract (slightly edited) is taken from, *The Necklace*, a short story by Guy de Maupassant (1850–1893). Read the extract and answer the questions which follow.

Background information

The story begins by immediately introducing the character of Madame Loisel.

She was one of those attractive pretty girls, born by a freak of fortune in a lower-middle-class family. She had no dowry, no expectations, no way of getting known, appreciated, loved and married by some wealthy gentleman of good family. And she allowed herself to be married to a junior clerk in the Ministry of Public Instruction.

She dressed plainly, having no money to spend on herself. But she was as unhappy as if she had known better days.

She always had a sense of frustration, feeling herself born for all the refinements and luxuries of life. She hated the bareness of her flat, the shabbiness of the walls, the worn upholstery of the chairs, and the ugliness of the curtains. All these things, which another woman of her class would not even have noticed, were pain and grief to her. The sight of the little Breton maid doing her simple house-work aroused in her passionate regrets and hopeless dreaming. She imagined hushed ante-rooms hung with oriental fabrics and lit by tall bronze candelabra, with two impressive footmen in knee-breeches dozing in great armchairs, made drowsy by the heat of the radiators. She imagined vast drawing-rooms, upholstered in antique silk, splendid pieces of furniture littered with priceless curios, and dainty scented boudoirs, designed for teatime conversation with intimate friends and much sought-after society gentlemen, whose attentions every woman envies and desires.

When she sat down to dinner at the round table covered with a three-days-old cloth opposite her husband, who took the lid off the casserole with the delighted exclamation: 'Ah! hot-pot again! How lovely! It's the best dish in the world!', she was dreaming of luxurious dinners with classical figures and exotic birds in a fair forest; she dreamt of exquisite dishes served on valuable china and whispered compliments listened to with a sphinx*-like smile while toying with the pink flesh of a trout or the wing of a hazel hen.

sphinx = a sphinx is an ancient Egyptian statue, having a woman's head and a lion's body

Questions

?

1. What impression of the character of Madame Loisel do you get from reading the extract? Give reasons for your answer.

2. What details in the extract suggest that this story is set in the nineteenth century rather than in a modern setting? Support your answer with specific details from the passage.

3. Explain the meaning of each of the following phrases:
   (a) born by a freak of fortune
   (b) littered with priceless curios
   (c) with a sphinx-like smile

4. What kind of person is Madame Loisel's husband, based on the evidence of the extract?

5. Name a character from a novel or short story you have studied who is disappointed or disillusioned for some reason. Explain what the reason for the disappointment is and how the character dealt with their situation. You must give the title of the novel or short story and the name of the author.

Using the PQE method to discuss a character from a studied novel:

Sample Question and Answer on Character

Select a character from a novel which you have studied who undergoes a change in the course of the narrative. Explain how this character changes.

The novel which I have studied is *To Kill a Mockingbird* by Harper Lee. Scout Finch, who is the narrator and one of the main characters, undergoes a journey of discovery about herself and her society in the course of the plot. At the start of the novel, Scout is only six years of age and has a naive and childish view of life. However, throughout the next three years of her life, she learns many important lessons which help her to grow up and become more mature.

One of these lessons is that people should be accepted for who they are and not treated with disrespect because they do things differently. **[P]** Calpurnia, the cook, insists on Scout treating Walter Cunningham with respect, even when he eats differently to the Finch family. She tells her crossly that she 'aint called on to contradict 'em . . . if he wants to eat up the tablecloth, you let him, you hear?'. Calpurnia will not tolerate Scout acting as if she were 'high and mighty' and accuses her of disgracing the family by commenting on Walter's request to pour molasses on his vegetables. This is an important lesson for Scout and one from which she learns. **[Q+E]**

Atticus also teaches Scout important lessons which bring about a change in her outlook on life and which make her change and grow up. **[P]** He encourages her to remain calm in heated situations and to avoid fighting as a means of venting her anger. He encourages her to try to see things from the point of view of others, telling her that she will 'never really understand a person' until she climbs 'into his skin' and 'walks around in it'. Although Scout has many problems heeding the advice of her father, she does learn these lessons and matures as the story progresses. **[Q+E]**

One of the most important lessons which Scout learns is that her society has the 'disease' of prejudice. **[P]** Scout learns that this prejudice is 'as much Maycomb as missionary teas' and comes to realise 'the simple hell people give other people.' She is not as insightful as her brother Jem, who is older than her, during the trial of Tom Robinson, naively believing that Tom must have been treated fairly. However, we see her growing maturity in the way that she understands that Boo Radley is not the monster that local ignorance and superstition have made him out to be. She learns that it would be 'sort of like shootin' a mockingbird' not to allow Boo the right to his privacy, although the local people would treat him like a hero for saving the lives of herself and Jem. **[Q+E]**

Throughout the novel, Scout learns many important lessons that help her to become more of a 'lady' and to behave with true courage and dignity. She still has a long way to go though and I found it very amusing when she remarked, at the end, that there wasn't much left for herself and Jem to learn, 'except, possibly, algebra'.

B. Setting

1. The Importance of Setting

The **setting** of a piece of literature is **the world** of the narrative; **a time and place** which provide a backdrop to the story. Setting can also include weather, historical period, a social environment and physical details about immediate surroundings. Settings can be realistic or imaginary (e.g. fantasy) or a combination of both real and imaginary elements. Most novels and short stories include more than one setting as the narrative progresses.

The function of the setting is of great importance in any narrative.

- It can have a huge effect on **plot** and **characters**.
- It can establish **mood** or **atmosphere**.
- It can add **realism** to a narrative.
- It can be **symbolic** in nature and related to central **themes**.
- It can help the reader to **engage imaginatively** with the characters and plot.

An author can bring the setting alive by using **descriptive details**. You need to ask yourself the following questions about setting:

- **Where** is this story taking place?
- What is the **importance** of the setting to the story?
- How does the writer use **language** to create the setting?

It is usually quite easy to establish the time and place of the setting. Sometimes writers give neutral, factual details which **convey objective information**:

> The town of Ballygarbh has a population of three thousand people. Many of the present inhabitants have lived in the town for most of their lives and can trace their roots back several centuries. Very few outsiders come to live in Ballygarbh, as it does not have much to offer as regards employment or opportunity. The old square, where people once congregated on fair days, is now home to a few small shops, a couple of pubs and a small filling station.

However, it can be more challenging to create a setting which **contributes to the narrative**. When commenting on setting, it is a good idea to ask yourself the following: What can I **see, hear, taste, feel, smell**? Writers can **appeal to the senses** to create a vivid sense of reality and invite the reader into the imagined world. Take, for example, the description of Maycomb in Harper Lee's *To Kill a Mockingbird*:

> Maycomb was an old town, but it was a tired old town when I first knew it. In rainy weather the streets turned to red slop; grass grew on the sidewalks, the courthouse sagged in the square. Somehow, it was hotter then; a black dog suffered on a summer's day; bony mules hitched to Hoover carts flicked flies in the sweltering shade of the live oaks on the square. Men's stiff collars wilted by nine in the morning. Ladies bathed before noon, after their three o' clock naps, and by nightfall were like soft tea-cakes with frostings of sweat and sweet talcum.
>
> People moved slowly then. They ambled across the square, shuffled in and out of the stores around it, took their time about everything. A day was twenty-four hours long but seemed longer. There was no hurry, for there was nowhere to go, nothing to buy and no money to buy it with.

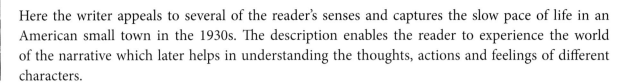

Here the writer appeals to several of the reader's senses and captures the slow pace of life in an American small town in the 1930s. The description enables the reader to experience the world of the narrative which later helps in understanding the thoughts, actions and feelings of different characters.

Word choice can help establish setting and mood. In the extract from *To Kill a Mockingbird* we can see some excellent examples of well-chosen words. Notice how the courthouse 'sagged', how men's collars 'wilted', how people 'ambled'. These verbs help to create the atmosphere of a place which could be unpleasant in both rainy and in 'sweltering' weather. The town is captured as being 'old' and 'tired', the people behave in a predictable manner and are set in their ways. All of these aspects become crucially important as events unfold because they influence the behaviour of the characters.

When you comment on how a writer creates setting, pay careful attention to **small details** and be prepared to comment on the writer's **word choice**.

2. Questions on Setting

Extract 1.

Read the opening lines from the novel, *The Picture of Dorian Grey*, by Oscar Wilde and answer the questions which follow.

The studio was filled with the rich odour of roses, and when the light summer wind stirred amidst the trees of the garden, there came through the open door the heavy scent of the lilac, or the more delicate perfume of the pink-flowering thorn.

Questions

1. Identify three phrases which appeal to our sense of smell and comment on the specific word choice in each phrase.
2. What details of the physical setting are revealed in this short extract?

Extract 2.

Read the extract from *A Farewell to Arms* by Ernest Hemingway and answer the questions that follow.

In the late summer of that year we lived in a house in a village that looked across the river and the plain to the mountains. In the bed of the river there were pebbles and boulders, dry and white in the sun, and the water was clear and swiftly moving and blue in the channels. Troops went by the house and down the road and the dust they raised powdered the leaves of the trees. The trunks of the trees too were dusty and the leaves fell early that year and we saw the troops marching along the road and the dust rising and leaves, stirred by the breeze, falling and the soldiers marching and afterward the road bare and white except for the leaves.

Questions

1. Which of the following sentences *best* describes the setting in this extract? Explain your choice.
   (a) The setting is in a remote and lonely place.
   (b) The setting is in a rural village.
   (c) The setting is near an army barracks.
   (d) The setting is in a house.
2. The author repeats the word 'and' very often in this description of the setting. In your opinion, what effect has this on the extract as a whole? Explain your response.
3. What senses are appealed to in this extract? You must support your answer with quotation from the extract.
4. What role does colour play in this description? Explain your answer.
5. How would you describe the atmosphere created in this extract? Give reasons for your answer.
6. Choose a description of a place from any novel or short story which you have read. Explain how the author created a sense of place and atmosphere. You must give the title of the text and name the author.

Extract 3.

Read the two extracts taken from the opening chapter of the novel *Wuthering Heights*, by Emily Brontë and answer the questions that follow.

'Wuthering Heights' is the name of Mr Heathcliff's dwelling. 'Wuthering' being a significant provincial adjective, descriptive of the atmospheric tumult to which its station is exposed in stormy weather. Pure, bracing ventilation they must have up there at all times, indeed: one may guess the power of the north wind blowing over the edge, by the excessive slant of a few stunted firs at the end of the house; and by a range of gaunt thorns all stretching their limbs one way, as if craving alms of the sun. Happily, the architect had foresight to build it strong: the narrow windows are deeply set in the wall, and the corners defended with large jutting stones.

Questions

1. Which of the following phrases best describes the location of 'Wuthering Heights'? Explain your choice of phrase with close reference to the descriptive details and language used by the author.
   (a) Remote and isolated
   (b) Rural and pretty
   (c) Fresh and invigorating
   (d) Harsh and bleak
   (e) Welcoming and friendly

2. What is the meaning, as used in the extract, of each of the following words:
   (a) Provincial
   (b) Atmospheric
   (c) Tumult
   (d) Bracing
   (e) Ventilation
   (f) Stunted
   (g) Jutting

3. Emily Brontë describes how the house is suited to its location: 'Happily, the architect had foresight to build it strong: the narrow windows are deeply set in the wall, and the corners defended with large jutting stones.' If this house is symbolic of Mr Heathcliff himself, what would you expect his main character traits to be?

The description continues as follows:

One stop brought us into the family sitting-room, without any introductory lobby or passage: they call it here 'the house' pre-eminently. It includes kitchen and parlour, generally; but I believe at Wuthering Heights the kitchen is <u>forced to retreat</u> altogether into another quarter: at least I distinguished a chatter of tongues, and a clatter of culinary utensils, deep within; and I observed no signs of roasting, boiling, or baking, about the huge fireplace; nor any glitter of copper saucepans and tin cullenders on the walls. One end, indeed, reflected splendidly both light and heat from ranks of immense pewter dishes, interspersed with silver jugs and tankards, towering row after row, on a vast oak dresser, to the very roof. The latter had never been under-drawn: its entire anatomy lay bare to an inquiring eye, except where a frame of wood laden with oatcakes and clusters of legs of beef, mutton, and ham, concealed it. Above the chimney were sundry <u>villainous old guns</u>, and <u>a couple of horse-pistols</u>: and, by way of ornament, three gaudily-painted canisters disposed along its ledge. The floor was of smooth, white stone; the chairs, high-backed, primitive structures, painted green: one or two heavy black ones <u>lurking</u> in the shade. In an arch under the dresser reposed a huge, liver-coloured bitch pointer, surrounded by a swarm of squealing puppies; and other dogs <u>haunted</u> other recesses.

Questions

1. Comment on each of the five underlined words or phrases in the above extract and suggest reasons why the author may have included them.
2. Identify descriptive details which appeal to our senses of sight (visual), hearing (aural) and touch (tactile).
3. What details suggest that the room is very large? Explain your response.
4. Basing your answer solely on these two extracts from *Wuthering Heights*, what do you think will be the major theme/themes of this novel? Give reasons for your answer.

Extract 4.

Read the extract from *White Fang* by Jack London and answer the questions that follow.

Dark spruce forest <u>frowned</u> on either side of the frozen waterway. The trees <u>had been stripped</u> by a recent wind of their white covering of frost, and they seemed to lean toward each other, black and ominous, in the fading light. A vast silence <u>reigned</u> over the land. The land itself was a desolation, lifeless, without movement, so lone and cold that the spirit of it was not even that of sadness. There was a hint in it of laughter, but of a laughter more terrible than any sadness

— a laughter that was mirthless as the smile of the Sphinx, a laughter cold as the frost and partaking of the grimness of infallibility. It was the masterful and incommunicable wisdom of eternity laughing at the futility of life and the effort of life. It was the Wild, the savage, frozen-hearted Northland Wild.

Questions

1. Find an example of each of the following techniques in the above paragraph and explain the effect of each in creating the setting:
   (a) Alliteration
   (b) Contrast
   (c) Repetition
   (d) Simile
   (e) Personification

2. Give a definition of each of the following words as used in the extract:
   (a) Ominous
   (b) Mirthless
   (c) Grimness
   (d) Infallibility
   (e) Incommunicable
   (f) Futility

3. How would you describe the atmosphere of this setting? Pay careful attention to sensual imagery and specific word choice in your answer.

4. Comment on the effect of the three underlined verbs in the extract.

5. Would this opening paragraph encourage you to read the entire novel? Give reasons why or why not.

Extract 5.

Read the extract from *The Haunting of Hill House* by Shirley Jackson and answer the questions that follow.

No live organism can continue for long to exist sanely under conditions of absolute reality; even larks and katydids* are supposed, by some, to dream. Hill House, not sane, stood by itself against its hills, holding darkness within; it had stood so for eighty years and might stand for eighty more. Within, walls continued upright, bricks met neatly, floors were firm, and doors were sensibly shut; silence lay steadily against the wood and stone of Hill House, and whatever walked there, walked alone…

katydids = a type of insect found in North America

Questions

1. How does the writer create a tense atmosphere in the description of the setting for this novel? Explain your response with detailed reference to the paragraph.

2. You have been asked to design a cover for this novel. Describe in detail what you would include in your design and why.

3. What do you think the author means when she describes Hill House as 'not sane'?

4. What do you think are the most important features of a good ghost story? Explain your choice of features.

5. Write the opening paragraph for a ghost story of your own. You might like to use some of the techniques used by Shirley Jackson in the extract.

6. The images below show the settings for three different stories. Choose one of the images and write a descriptive paragraph in which you create a picture of the place and give the reader a sense of the mood or atmosphere of that place.

2. 'The Wishing Lamp'

1. 'The Journey Home'

3. 'First Performance'

C. Plot

1. Analysing Plot

The plot refers to the **sequence of events** or the **shape** that a story takes. One could imagine it as a sort of map for a journey which the reader takes during the course of the narrative.

When planning the plot of a narrative, the writer has to make certain decisions. You should examine the following questions in the short stories and novels you have studied:

■ How is the **time sequence** handled? Is there a **chronological order**, where the writer works progressively through the events as they occur, or is there a **flashback** or a series of flashbacks, which shape the narrative?

■ How and when are **new characters** introduced? What **complications** and **obstacles** arise for the main characters, which make us want to read on to find out what is going to happen?

■ How is **conflict** and **tension** created? Suspense is a prime ingredient of any story and is necessary to maintain the reader's interest. Suspense comes from the building up of tension, keeping the reader in a state of heightened anxiety or uncertainty. It may rely on conflicts or tensions between the characters themselves, conflicts or tensions surrounding events, or tensions relating to the setting, e.g. a battlefield or a haunted house. The important ingredient is that **the reader is left uncertain about what will happen and wants to read on to find out**.

■ **Climax** may be described as a series of events, increasing in tension until a critical point is reached. It is usually the **turning point** in a story and leads to the conclusion. Where does the story come to a climax? Is there more than one climax? Ask yourself where the story has been going – follow the 'map'.

   Take for example the climax in Steinbeck's novel *Of Mice and Men*. George is about to kill his close friend Lennie to spare him from a lynch mob. The two friends engage in a dialogue about the dream they shared to own their own home. As Lennie looks across the river, George brings the novel to its climax:

> '. . . George raised the gun and steadied it, and he brought the muzzle of it close to the back of Lennie's head. The hand shook violently, but his face set and his hand steadied. He pulled the trigger. The crash of the shot rolled up the hills and rolled down again. Lennie jarred, and then settled slowly forward to the sand, and he lay without quivering.

■ How does the **pace** vary? It is important to have changes in the speed at which events happen. Too much dialogue slows the action down, but enough must be given to make the characters seem real. Likewise, too many events happening in quick succession, or the plot lurching from one crisis to another creates a sense of unreality.

■ How does the conflict **resolve**? Remember, there may be more than one conflict in a novel. What happens as a result of the resolution of the conflict? How does the story end?

2. Mapping the Plot

To ensure that you understand the shape of the plot of any text you have studied, you should create a 'map' of the sequence of events and label each stage clearly.

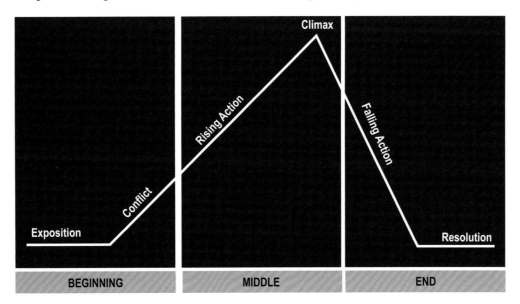

D. Theme

1. The Central Idea in Fiction

A theme is a **central idea** that provides the inspiration for a plot. A short story normally develops one theme, whereas a novel may have several themes. Themes may focus on such things as prejudice, war, love, loyalty, ambition, etc. Most aspects of human life can provide the writer with a theme on which to base a plot. Themes provide a springboard for the plot and give meaning to the lives and relationships of the characters.

You should be able to answer the following questions about themes:

- How does the theme emerge from the **actions and dialogue** of the characters? You should be able to trace a theme or themes from beginning to end.
- How do the major **events** bring out the theme?
- How does the **setting** contribute to the theme? Examine the setting carefully, after you have identified the theme, and ask yourself if the setting has an important role to play in bringing out the theme.
- How does the **language and imagery** contribute to the theme? Descriptive details and specific word choice can indicate or highlight the theme. Be on the lookout for language which appeals to the senses and examine any symbols or other images to see how they influence the theme.

Read this extract as an example of how a theme can be traced through a narrative extract. It is taken from the novel *Remembrance* by Theresa Breslin. Francis, a soldier, is writing to his friend Maggie. In this letter he shares with her his experiences of the trenches of World War 1.

My dear Maggie,

We came up from our rest billet the other night to relieve the troops in the front lines. I swear the times of our movements must be known to our enemies for they <u>shelled the road</u> as soon as we began, and stopped immediately we reached the communications trenches. We left the road at once and <u>crawled</u> through an orchard and some pigpens to reach our destination by another route. <u>It seems incredible, but among this devastation the trees here are beginning to</u>

bud – after a bitter winter, spring now struggles to break through. As the thaw sets in it is the most punishing work to keep the trenches free of water. The pumps are poor excuses, and barely work. Our engineers have designed crude constructions which they call "duckboards" – long square poles of wood with thick crossbars set at intervals. These are made from whatever can be requisitioned, stolen or scavenged. Wood from shelled and bombed buildings, empty ration crates, wattle fencing, anything and everything is used.

My "hotel" view at the moment is out across the stretch of earth they call No Man's Land and the very phrase sums up the waste of war – there is a solitary tree stripped of life and colour, spent ammunition, shrapnel and shell and . . . the unburied dead.

I am strangely unafraid of death; there is a trance-like quality to life under these circumstances. What frightens me more is the death of spirit, that I have so quickly become accustomed to the sights and sounds of war . . . such an ache in my head and in my heart.

Francis

billet = a place for soldiers to lodge

The theme of war, its suffering and waste, is very carefully traced throughout. The speaker in the extract recounts the actions of the soldiers in some detail as they make their way to the trenches. The underlined words and sentences illustrate the use that can be made of **action, setting, language** and **imagery** to bring out the dominant theme that war is a waste of life, which can also kill the human spirit.

2. Questions on Theme

Sample Questions and Answers on Theme

1. **What is meant by a theme in a narrative text?**

   The theme in a narrative text refers to the overall meaning, message or central idea of a story.

2. **Select a novel or short story you have studied which has an interesting theme and write an outline of how the theme emerges in the plot.**

   A short story which I have read and which has an interesting theme is 'The Majesty of the Law' by Frank O'Connor. The theme of legal justice develops in an unusual way in this story.

   The theme is introduced when Dan Bride, who lives alone in a cottage, has a visit from a sergeant. Dan has prepared whiskey, tea and bread to offer his guest – 'a sure sign that he had been expecting a visitor'. The sergeant is supposed to uphold law and order but has no problem in drinking the illegal whiskey, even going so far as to say that he does not agree with the law which bans the practice.

   Later, the sergeant asks Dan if he is willing to pay a fine which he owes. Dan refuses as he does not want to give 'that fellow' the satisfaction. The sergeant then produces a warrant for his arrest. This entire exchange takes place in a polite and respectful manner. The sergeant suggests that others are willing to pay Dan's fine if he cannot afford to pay it himself. Rather than grasping at the opportunity to escape imprisonment, Dan refers to the warrant as an 'unneighbourly document' and chooses to go to prison.

It is not until the end of the story that we discover what offence Dan has been accused of; he 'had the grave misfortune to open the head of another old man', who had to be hospitalised. There is no doubt that Dan wants to go to jail in order to embarrass his victim and not because it is legally and morally just that he pays for his crime. He knows that his neighbours will support him, which they do, and that the old man will be punished for seeking justice.

The story ends with the victim having to scurry indoors to hide from the group of Dan's friends who are openly shaking his hand and offering him support.

3. **As the theme develops why does it interest you? Support your answer with reference to your chosen novel or short story.** (You can use the Point, Quote, Explain technique for this answer.)

This theme developed in a way which held my interest right up to the final sentence. The fact that I did not know the reason for the sergeant's visit, but guessed from the title that it had something to do with the law, made me want to read on. **[P]**

It came as a bit of a shock to discover that a man, suffering from arthritis and as old as Dan Bride could be capable of splitting open the head of another old man in the course of a row. **[P]** This was not a 'grave misfortune', it was an assault which left the victim 'hospitalised'. I found it very interesting to observe the attitude of the sergeant. I would have expected a more abrupt and official manner, not bread and tea and plenty of small talk! **[Q+E]**

There is also something very interesting in the fact that Dan is allowed to choose the day he will go to jail. **[P]** That is not usual for somebody who has committed a serious, violent crime. The fact that the sergeant is treating Dan so politely is nothing short of astonishing. He even tells Dan that he will ensure that he is made 'as comfortable as if you were at home' while he is in prison. This sergeant, who drinks illegally made alcohol with Dan, certainly has an extraordinary attitude to law and order! I began to wonder about the majesty of the law, which seems to condone violence. **[Q+E]**

Of most interest, however, is the reaction of Dan's neighbours. **[P]** Not only are they willing to pay his fine but they shake his hand before he is taken away. This sympathy shows an interesting attitude to the law and how the people view justice. Although I sympathised with Dan – he was not a wealthy man and had been cheated by the other individual – I still found it fascinating that the community would condone his violent behaviour. In the end, the old man who was assaulted is left feeling ashamed that he set the law on 'one of his own'. **[Q+E]**

I found it very curious that Dan's assault on a man who cheated him was seen as a lesser crime than that committed by his victim. The whole story questions the notion of what constitutes legal, impartial justice.

E. Style

1. How Style is Created

The style of a narrative refers to the **way it is written**. It includes how characters, setting and atmosphere are created. It also includes the way in which the writer uses dialogue, language and imagery. These have already been covered in this unit. However, you also need to examine and be aware of:

- How the writer uses **verbs** to provide insight into character and assist atmosphere. For example, let us take the extract from *Of Mice and Men* already referred to:

> . . . George <u>raised</u> the gun and <u>steadied</u> it, and he brought the muzzle of it close to the back of Lennie's head. The hand <u>shook</u> violently, but his face <u>set</u> and his hand <u>steadied</u>. He <u>pulled</u> the trigger. The crash of the shot <u>rolled</u> up the hills and rolled down again. Lennie <u>jarred</u>, and then <u>settled</u> slowly forward to the sand, and he <u>lay</u> without quivering.

The verbs underlined are carefully selected and are crucial in showing us that George does not want to shoot Lennie. He has difficulty in carrying out the act. This shows his love and loyalty to his friend and his conflict at that moment. The atmosphere is tense and dramatic as George steadies the gun, shakes and steadies himself again before pulling the trigger. The repetition of the verb 'rolled', creates an atmosphere of the exploding, reverberating sound of the gunshot. Lennie's body did not just 'fall' – it 'jarred' and 'settled'. Always examine how a writer uses verbs in a passage and be able to comment on their effect.

- Note the **point of view** of the narrative. Ask yourself if it is written in the first person (I, we) or the third person (he, she, they). As we have already seen, the use of the first person makes the narrative more immediate to the reader and allows the reader to view characters and events from the narrator's subjective perspective. The use of the third person or the omniscient (all-knowing) viewpoint allows for greater insight into the minds and thoughts of other characters and creates a more objective viewpoint

- Narratives are usually written in the past tense, but the present tense is also used effectively in some stories. Examine the **verb tense** in the passage you are describing and note if the writer suddenly changes tense. This usually indicates that something important or noteworthy is happening.

- Note how the writer carefully chooses **adjectives** and **adverbs**. These must be used carefully to bring the story alive, qualify the action and provide description and information for the reader.

- Pay particular attention to how the writer uses **images** which appeal to the senses. We have seen an example of this in the extract from *To Kill a Mockingbird*, but every narrative will provide plenty of examples of such images.

- It is important to recognise and be able to comment on any use of **simile**, **metaphor** or **symbol** used in the text. Be also on the lookout for **personification**, which can create dramatic effects.

- Look carefully at the **details** in descriptions. Ask yourself why the writer is describing someone or something in such detail. Pay attention to **specific words** and ask yourself why they have been selected by the writer.

- Examine how the writer varies **sentence structure**. Check the paragraphs to get a sense of how many sentences are short or abrupt, how many are long and complex and how many are questions or exclamations. Good writers usually vary their sentence structure.

- **Humour** is a feature of style which engages and entertains the reader. Humour can be used simply to make the reader laugh; it can also be used in a cynical or dark manner to highlight serious themes.

2. Beginnings and Endings

If you understand a writer's style, you won't have a problem matching the opening of a narrative text with its conclusion.

Beginnings

Opening paragraphs have several important functions:

- **They serve as a 'hook' to grab the reader's attention.** It is very important to grab the reader's attention from the outset. Many writers achieve this by using language in an unusual or dramatic way or by establishing a unique narrative voice. A surprising piece of dialogue or a startling action can also intrigue the reader and draw them into the story. Whatever method is used, its main function is to encourage the reader to read on.

- **They place the reader in a world or setting.** The reader needs to know when and where the story is taking place. Some writers describe the setting or set up an atmosphere at the beginning of the narrative. Certain sensory details give clues about the location, even if we are not told where we are in the first couple of paragraphs.

- **They intrigue the reader by presenting a character or group of characters.** Characters need to be interesting or unusual in some way if the reader is going to engage with them for the entire novel.

- **They create questions which the reader wants answered.** A conflict or puzzle needs to be introduced early in the plot to encourage the reader to want to find out what happens next.

Bearing the above points in mind, examine the opening paragraphs from *The Killing Woods* by Lucy Christopher and answer the questions that follow.

Something was draped across Dad's outstretched arms.

A deer? A fawn that was injured? It was sprawled and long-legged, something that had been caught in a poacher's trap maybe. A mistake. So this is where Dad had been all this time: in the woods and cutting this creature free. I breathed out slowly, squinted at the mist that hovered around Dad like a ghost. I took my hand from my bedroom window, leaving the memory of my skin on the glass. Then I raced down the stairs, through the hall and into the kitchen out back. Throwing open the door to the garden, I waited for him there.

It was ages since Dad had brought back something injured, and he'd never brought back a deer, though I could remember helping him free a roe deer from a snare in the woods once. Back then his hands had moved quickly and gently, darting from the wire on the doe's leg and then to her neck for a pulse, stroking her constantly.

This was something like that again. Saving another deer could be a good thing for Dad, something to take his mind off everything else, to help bring him out of his dark place.

I heard Dad's feet scuff on the cobbles in the lane, saw his movement. I tried to pick out the shape of the deer's body, but it was all wrong. The legs weren't long enough, neither was its neck. I took a step towards them. And that's when it made sense: the shape.

It wasn't a deer Dad was carrying. It was a girl.

Questions

1. How does the writer hook the reader's interest in the first sentence of the novel?

2. What effect is created by the use of rhetorical questions?

3. What kind of person is the narrator from the evidence given in this passage? Explain your response.

4. Why, in your opinion, is the narrator so concerned about her father? Refer to details in the text when answering.

5. How does the writer create setting and atmosphere in these opening paragraphs? Refer to specific details to support your answer.

6. What puzzles or mysteries emerge in these opening paragraphs?

7. Having read this opening section, would you like to read the whole novel? Explain why or why not.

8. Give the titles and authors of two novels which you have studied. Using the opening section of each text, explain the techniques used by each author to 'hook' the reader.

9. Which of the openings of your studied novels did you find the most engaging? Give reasons for your answer.

10. Write an opening paragraph which would be suitable for a mystery novel.

Middles

The middle of a story involves a series of events or complications which have important functions:

- **They increase the tension** for the reader.
- As the story evolves, we get **a deeper insight into the characters**, observing how they grow and change as they confront various **obstacles** or **conflicts**.
- Although some of the earlier, minor crises are resolved to some extent, the story continues until it reaches a **major crisis** or **climax**.

Endings

At the end of a narrative the main conflict is resolved and any **loose ends are tied up**. Although the **tension falls** quickly, a good ending leaves the reader satisfied that the story is complete even if they are disappointed with the way things turned out.

Endings usually come quite quickly after the main climax. Given that it is the desire to know what is going to happen next which keeps the reader engaged, there is not much to maintain interest after the climax, which usually answers most of the reader's questions about the outcome of the plot.

A good ending has one or more of the following features:

- They show (or suggest) the result of the story's conflict.
- They are related to the actions of the main character/s.
- They use material from the story's beginning and middle sections.
- They make the reader feel something.
- They make the reader think about some issue.
- They give a sense of satisfaction and completion.

A very simple example of the relationship between the middle and the ending of a story can be seen in the children's fairytale of *The Three Little Pigs*. After the **introduction** of the three pigs and their decisions to build houses, **tension builds** up each time that the wolf manages to blow a house down. The wolf's inability to blow down the house made of bricks **resolves a crisis** until the wolf decides to come down the chimney instead. Tension builds until the **climax** is reached when the wolf falls into the pot of boiling water. The **ending** of the story quickly follows as the scalded wolf either dies in the pot or races away, never to be seen again.

Novels and short stories are far more complex and subtle than a child's fairytale, but the same narrative curve or arc occurs. The story begins, becomes more complex until it reaches a climax and then moves quickly to its conclusion.

Questions and Sample Answers on Beginnings and Endings

Junior Cycle 20XX Sample 2

The beginnings of three novels are presented below.

The endings of the same three novels, plus one additional ending, are on the next page. The endings are not necessarily in the same order as the beginnings.

Read all of the beginnings and endings and then answer the questions that follow.

Beginnings

Beginning A

Some people used to believe that there was an elephant graveyard – a place that sick and old elephants would travel to die. They'd slip away from their herds and would lumber across the dusty landscape, like the titans we read about in Greek Mythology. Legend said the spot was in Saudi Arabia; that is was the source of a supernatural force; that it contained a book of spells to bring about world peace. Explorers who went in search of the graveyard would follow dying elephants for weeks, only to realize they'd been led in circles. Some of these voyagers disappeared completely. Some could not remember what they had seen, and not a single explorer who claimed to have found the elephant graveyard could ever locate it again.

Here's why: the the elephant graveyard is a myth.

Beginning B

He was an old man who fished alone in a skiff in the Gulf Stream and he had gone eighty-four days now without taking a fish. In the first forty days a boy had been with him. But after forty days without a fish the boy's parents had told him that the old man was now definitely and finally salao, which is the worst form of unlucky, and the boy had gone at their orders in another boat which caught three good fish the first week. It made the boy sad to see the old man come in each day with the skiff empty and he always went down to help him carry either the coiled lines or the gaff and harpoon and the sail that was furled around the mast. The sail was patched with flour sacks and, furled, it looked like the flag of permanent defeat.

Beginning C

MAE MOBLEY was born on a early Sunday morning in August 1960. A church baby we like to call it. Taking care a white babies, that's what I do, along with all the cooking and cleaning. I done raised seventeen kids in my lifetime. I even know how to get them babies to sleep, stop crying, and go in the toilet bowl before they mamas even get out abed in the morning.

Endings

Ending 1

That afternoon there was a party of tourists at the terrace and looking down in the water among the empty beer cans and dead barracudas a woman saw a great long white spine with a huge tail at the end that lifted and swung with the tide while the east wind blew a heavy steady sea outside the entrance to the harbor.

'What's that?' she asked a waiter and pointed to the long back bone of the great fish.

'Tiburon,' the waiter said, 'Shark.' He was meaning to explain what had happened.

'I didn't know sharks had such handsome beautifully formed tails.'

Up the road, in his shack, the old man was sleeping again. He was still sleeping on his face and the boy was sitting by him watching him. The old man was dreaming about the lions.

Ending 2

The sun is bright but my eyes is wide open. I stand at the bus stop like I been doing for forty-odd years. In thirty years, my whole life's done. Maybe I ought to keep writing, not just for the paper, but something else, about all the people I know and the things I seen and done. Maybe I ain't too old to start over, I think and I laugh and I cry at the same time at this. Cause just last night I thought I was finished with everything new.

Ending 3

When Lawrence Anthony died, the two herds travelled through the Zululand Bush for more than half a day and stood outside the wall that bordered his property. They had not been near the house in over a year. The elephants stayed for two days, silent, bearing witness.

No one can explain how the elephants knew that Anthony had died.

I know the answer.

If you think about someone you've loved and lost, you are already with them. The rest is just details.

Ending 4

Then he was gone, walking slowly round the shore in the half-light. The Ruttledges did not speak as they climbed the hill.

'What are you going to do?' Kate asked as they passed beneath the alder tree.

'I'm not sure.' he said. 'We can talk it through. We don't have to decide on anything til morning.'

At the porch, before entering the house, they both turned to look back across the lake, even though they knew that both Jamesie and Mary had long since disappeared from the sky.

1. **For each of the three beginnings, select which of the endings (1,2,3,4) you think is the correct one.**

Beginning	Ending
A	3
B	1
C	2

2. **In the case of Beginning B and Beginning C, justify your selection, based on both the content and the style of each extract.**

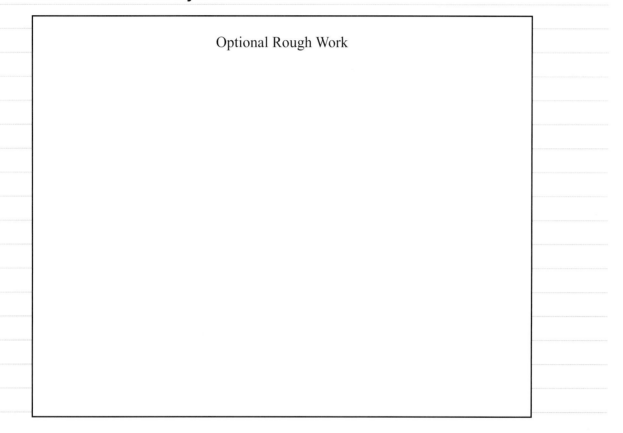

Optional Rough Work

Beginning B – Justification of chosen ending:

I think Ending 1 matches with Beginning B for a few reasons. The first reason is setting. 'B' opens on a fishing community, and '1' ends with scenes of great fish and barracudas. Another reason is the characters: 'B' features a boy and an old man, as does '1'. Finally, the style is third person narrative. This could relate to Beginning A and B, but B's style is simpler and less academic-sounding than A. This simple style is reflected in Ending 1.

Beginning C – Justification of chosen ending:

Beginning C is the only opening that is told in the first person. The language sounds like black American dialect; I think this because she makes a point of saying she takes care of 'white babies' and makes certain grammatical errors like 'I done raised' and 'before they mamas'. Ending 2 is told in the same voice, with statements like, 'my eyes is wide open'. There's a confessional style to the two excerpts, like someone letting us into her private life.

3. **Write a definition of each word as it is used in its passage.**

   <u>Lumber:</u> To walk heavily or gracelessly at a slow pace.

   <u>Furled:</u>   To curl up or roll something neatly so it is packed away for later use.

   <u>Witness:</u> To see something significant happen and not interfere.

   <u>Legend:</u> An old story, not always true, that people tell about a famous event or person.

   <u>Terrace:</u> A step or patio, sometimes built on a slope, where people can relax.

4. **List any three characteristics that you believe are important for a good opening to a novel.**

   1. *I think a good opening to a novel should introduce us to a distinct world, so <u>setting</u> is important. If the reader can get a sense of where the action takes place, and the more vivid and real that world feels (even if it is a fantastical world) then it affects the reader more powerfully.*

   2. *Good <u>characterisation</u> is essential. The opening of a novel should introduce us to a character or group of characters who create interest and engage us so that we want to continue reading.*

   3. *I believe that <u>language</u> is very important in the opening of a novel. I like the language of novels I read to be direct and fast-moving. Vivid verb choice keeps the action sharp and clear, and I prefer not to get too bogged down in flowery description. It's important that the language in the opening paragraphs reflects the language of the entire novel.*

Responding to texts

The beginnings of three narratives are presented below. The endings of the same three narratives and one additional ending follow. Read all of the beginnings and endings and then answer the questions 1–5 on page 124.

Beginning A

It was a day of holocausts, cataclysms, tornadoes, earthquakes, blackouts, mass murders, eruptions, and miscellaneous dooms, at the peak of which the sun swallowed the earth and the stars vanished.

But to put it simply, the most respected member of the Bentley family up and died.

Dog was his name, and dog he was.

The Bentleys, arising late Saturday morning, found Dog stretched on the kitchen floor, his head toward Mecca, his paws neatly folded, his tail not a-thump but silent for the first time in twenty years.

Beginning B

The ghost that got into our house on the night of November 17, 1915, raised such a hullabaloo of misunderstandings that I am sorry I didn't just let it keep on walking, and go to bed. Its advent caused my mother to throw a shoe through a window of the house next door and ended up with my grandfather shooting a patrolman. I am sorry, therefore, as I have said, that I ever paid any attention to the footsteps.

Beginning C

Without, the night was cold and wet, but in the small parlour of Laburnum Villa the blinds were drawn and the fire burned brightly. Father and son were at chess; the former, who possessed ideas about the game involving radical changes, putting his king into such sharp and unnecessary perils that it even provoked comment from the white-haired old lady knitting placidly by the fire.

Ending 1

Grandfather was fresh as a daisy and full of jokes at breakfast next morning. We thought at first he had forgotten all about what had happened, but he hadn't. Over his third cup of coffee, he glared at Herman and me. 'What was the idee of all them cops tarryhootin' round the house last night?' he demanded. He had us there.

Ending 2

That night Jack Murphy slept the sleep of the just. In the morning he received his breakfast in bed. His wife sat on the edge fondly watching him as he ate.

'I have good news for you', she said.

'What would that be?' Jack asked absently.

'You needn't bother to return the other coat. Margaretta thinks it a steal at twenty-five pounds and she's decided to keep it.'

Ending 3

Everyone turned.

A strange man stood in the door holding a small wicker basket from which came familiar, small yapping sounds.

And even as the flames from the candles around the coffin caught the curtains and the last sparks blew on the wind, the whole family, drawn out into the sunlight, gathered around the stranger with the wicker basket, waiting for father to arrive to throw back the coverlet on the small carrier so they could all dip their hands in.

That moment, as Susan said later, was like reading the telephone book one more time.

Ending 4

The knocking ceased suddenly, although the echoes of it were still in the house. He heard the chair drawn back, and the door opened. A cold wind rushed up the staircase, and a long loud wail of disappointment and misery from his wife gave him courage to run down to her side, and then to the gate beyond. The street lamp flickering opposite shone on a quiet and deserted road.

Questions

1. For each of the three beginnings, select which of the endings 1, 2, 3 or 4 you think is the correct one.

   (a) Beginning A = Ending _____

   (b) Beginning B = Ending _____

   (c) Beginning C = Ending _____

2. In the case of each beginning and ending, justify your selection, based on both the content and style of each extract.

3. List any three characteristics that you believe are important for a good opening to a novel or short story.

4. List any three characteristics that you believe are important to a good ending to a novel or story.

5. Using the criteria that you suggested in your responses to 3 and 4 above, write an assessment of the opening and closing sections of any novel studied by you for your coursework. You must give the title of the novel and the name of the author.

F. Answering Questions on Fiction

1. Types of Exam Questions

Questions can take various formats but you may be specifically asked to:

- Comment on **characters**. Be able to form impressions about the characters, their relationships and their motives from reading what is said about them, what they say about themselves or others and, most importantly, what they do. Pay special attention to any dialogue.

- Comment on **setting**. You might be asked how the setting affects the passage given in the unseen extract or how it affects the novel or short stories you have studied.

- Comment on **theme**. From your reading of the narrative, what main idea or ideas are driving the plot? Be prepared to give evidence to support your views.

- Comment on **atmosphere** and how it is created. This is a **style** question.

- Comment on a **key moment**. This could be any event leading up to the climax or be the actual climax of the narrative.

- Comment on the **opening or the closing sections** in studied fiction. You will be expected to have opinions about these sections or chapters and be able to discuss the effect they had on you as a reader.

- Imagine that you are one of the characters and write a **diary entry** or a **letter**. You might be asked to recount events from the point of view of a particular character.

2. Answering on Unseen Fiction

- Read the unseen fiction extract very carefully and analyse any tasks or questions before you write your response.

- If there is an introduction to the extract, read it carefully. This will give you a general idea of the setting.

- Now read the questions very carefully. Highlight the important words in each question and make sure that you do not leave out any part of the questions.

- Beginning with the first question, read over the extract again marking off any words or phrases which you think will be useful as support for your response. Keep asking yourself questions. For example, if you are asked what impression you got of a person or a relationship, ask yourself why you got that impression, what words created it, why did the writer pick certain words, etc. This will help to give your response a sharp focus.

- Write your answer. Answers will vary in length, but they must be relevant to the question asked. If you find yourself telling the story to the reader – STOP! You are probably moving away from the question. Check again to see what the question asked you to do. Now continue your answer, keeping an eye on exactly what you have been asked.

- Some questions might require you to support your points with quotation from, or reference to, the extract. Choose quotations carefully. It may be that a few words or a short phrase will illustrate the point you are making. Avoid writing out big chunks of the text.

- If you are asked for your opinion, or to form an impression, make sure that you respond personally when answering and that you explain your reasons for your opinion or impression.

3. Answering on Studied Fiction

- The questions in this section will allow you to show your knowledge of and response to the novels or short stories studied during your Junior Cycle.

- Revise the **Key Skills For Answering on Fiction**, which are listed on page 93.

- Make sure that you can discuss the characters, setting, plot, themes and style of your chosen texts. Be able to demonstrate the part played by each of these elements in the narrative.

Advice

- Prepare your novel or short stories well in advance. Pay particular attention to key chapters or sections of the narratives. This will put you in a strong position to answer well in the exam.

- Practise writing answers following the P.Q.E. method where suitable. As you improve with practice, you will find that you can think, plan and write quickly.

- Keep strictly within the time-limits. If you find that you simply cannot write the same length as the samples provided in this section, shorten your quotes and explanations.

Use the following checklist to ensure that you have complied with the demands of the exam paper's marking scheme:

1. Have I practised writing both unseen and studied questions on fiction? ☐

2. Have I prepared my texts carefully following the guidelines for analysing fiction? ☐

3. Have I read the questions very carefully and ensured that I am addressing all parts of the questions? ☐

4. Have I underlined the key words in all questions before choosing a question to answer? ☐

5. Have I made a short plan, ensuring that I am addressing the question? ☐

6. Have I made relevant points and supported them with quotation? ☐

7. Have I offered some explanation of my points? ☐

8. Have I made some personal comments in the course of my answer? ☐

9. Have I paragraphed properly, developing one point in each paragraph? ☐

10. Have I checked my spelling, punctuation and grammar? ☐

If you can tick each of these boxes, you will be able to answer questions on both studied and unseen fiction.

04 Literacy

Learning Outcomes

This unit addresses the following learning outcomes:
OL8, 12, R1, 2, 13; W1, 3, 4, 6, 7, 9.

Introduction

To demonstrate your competence in social literacy, you must be aware of the content to be communicated, the correct structure and the form of expression appropriate to the audience being addressed. In oral literacy and visual literacy for the Final Assessment Examination, students are expected to be able to: interpret meaning, compare, evaluate effectiveness of, and respond to drama, poetry, media broadcasts, digital media, images and oral language, noting key ideas, style, tone, content and overall impact in a systematic way.

The Key Skills for social literacy are:

1. Well-structured answers.
2. Clarity of expression.
3. Use of an appropriate tone.
4. Good grammar, spelling and punctuation.

A. Social Literacy

1. Letters and Emails

The most important element of writing a good letter or email is your ability to identify and write to your audience. Letters and emails can be **formal** or **informal**. Formal letters are business letters. Informal letters are written to friends, relatives or people you know well.

(a) Formal letters

There are different kinds of formal letters. Here are some examples:
- letters of complaint
- letters of application for jobs
- letters of invitation to a formal event
- letters to the editor of a newspaper

Guidelines for writing a formal letter:

1. Before you begin, ask yourself the following questions: **Who** am I writing to? **Why** am I writing? **What** do I need to tell them? **What** do I want them to do?
2. The language used should be **formal and business-like**. Avoid slang or colloquial language. Do not use abbreviations or contractions. Emotional language or sarcasm should be avoided.
3. The **purpose of the letter** should be absolutely clear to the recipient. You should state the purpose of the letter in your opening paragraph – after the opening salutation / greeting.
4. The letter should be **concise**. Do not use long, rambling sentences or lose sight of the purpose of your writing. Do not be vague about your objective just get to the point without going into unnecessary details.
5. The letter should be **organised in a logical manner**. All letters follow a standard format, see below.
6. Your **spelling and grammar** should be free from errors. So re-read very carefully!

Format for a formal letter:

Read these guidelines and check them against the letter below.

1. **Your address** should be displayed in the **top right hand corner**.
2. The **date** should be displayed just **below your address on the right**. Skip a line between your address and the date. Give full date e.g. 26th March 2020. Avoid abbreviations.
3. **The name / title and address of the person you are writing to** should be displayed on the **left hand side of the letter** – just below the level of your own address.
4. The **formal salutation or greeting** should be below the name and address of the recipient. Skip a line. When you know the name of the person you are writing to, you open by formally addressing them: Dear Ms Collins. If you do not know the recipient's name, address them as Dear Sir / Madam.
5. The **opening paragraph** should clearly state the **purpose** of the letter.
6. The following two or three paragraphs should form **the body of the letter** – each paragraph developing **one major point or comment**.
7. The **final paragraph** should conclude the letter.
8. **Close formally** by using the words, Yours sincerely **if you know the name of the person you are writing to or** Yours faithfully **if you do not know their name**.
9. **Sign your name.** (write your name in block capitals underneath your signature).

Sample letter of complaint

1 56 Fairtree Road,
Bridgewater,
Cork.

2 10th March 2020

3 Mr John Mitchell,
52 Fairtree Road,
Bridgewater,
Cork

4 Dear Mr Mitchell,

5 I am writing to you concerning the nuisance created by your dogs barking at night.

6 As you are well aware, I have asked you repeatedly to bring your dogs indoors after 11.00 p.m. which I do not consider to be an unreasonable request. However, despite your assurance that you would do so, you have allowed the animals to remain outdoors, barking at passing pedestrians and road traffic.

Not only am I wakened during the night by your dogs, but so are my children, one of whom is a baby. Several other neighbours also have young children who are being disturbed. This clearly cannot be allowed to continue.

I would very much appreciate if you would take immediate steps to rectify this matter. Failing any satisfactory response to this request, I will have no option but to contact the Garda Síochána and make a formal complaint.

7 I hope you will carefully consider and respond positively to this request as it is in everybody's interest to maintain pleasant neighbourhood relationships.

8 Yours sincerely,

9 Michael Barrett
MICHAEL BARRETT

Tasks

1. Imagine that John Mitchell calls over to Michael Barrett's house after receiving the letter. Write out the conversation that takes place between them. Set your answer out in script format and indicate in brackets the appropriate use of body language, gestures etc. The opening lines are as follows:

JM: I received this letter (*waving it in MB's face*) in this morning's post and I must say that I'm very annoyed by your attitude to my dogs. What kind of dogs don't bark? What's all this talk of calling the Guards? (*Aggressively stands with his arms folded and a scowl appearing on his face*)

MB: (*Speaking calmly and slowly*) If you would read my letter properly, you would see that it's the barking <u>at night</u> (*with emphasis*) that is the problem. (*He opens door and politely gestures to JM to enter*) Would you like to step into the house and we could perhaps discuss this civilly?

WOOOF

2. The letter below is an invitation to a person to speak at a conference. Unfortunately, the writer is not clear about the correct way to write a formal letter. Several things need to be deleted, inserted or re-phrased. Rewrite the letter correctly. You may like to use some of the words or phrases in the box below the letter.

The Young Writers' Centre,
Parnell Square,
Dublin 1.

Mr John Holloway,
'The Moorings',
Dalkey,
County Dublin.

Hi Mr Holloway,

I am writing for the above writing centre to formally invite you to speak at our forthcoming conference on 'Young Irish Writing Today'.

This conference will take place in The Highbury Hotel, Abbey Street, Dublin on 15th June 2020, starting at 10.00 a.m. and it'll be over at 5.30.p.m. Hope you'll able to accept our invitation, we'll be more than happy to offer you the speaking time of your choice. Maybe you'd speak for approximately one hour. That'd be great.

The conference hopes to raise awareness of the talents possessed by aspiring young writers, some of them will read excerpts from their own work. We hope that there will be lively discussion and feedback from the audience. As well as that, we want to assist young writers by inviting writers the likes of yourself to offer advice and share insights into the art of writing right.

As a voluntary group, we cannot, unfortunately, pay you loads, but we would cough up your travel expenses and get ready a mid-day lunch and evening dinner for you.

We would be so chuffed if you could attend and speak at our conference.

I can be contacted at the above address or at the telephone or email address below.

Bye for now,

Michael Andrews.

Secretary: 'The Young Writer's Centre'
Telephone: 01 9487263
email: m.andrews@gmail.net

---

provide – it is proposed that – of your calibre and distinction – reimburse –
effectively – pay a large fee – you will – that would – in addition – we will
– some of whom – honoured and grateful – Dear – concluding

(b) Business emails

Guidelines for writing a business email:

1. **Give the message a subject:** The subject line is the mini-summary of your email. It provides the biggest opportunity to ensure your email gets read. Keep the subject short and clear.

2. **Opening/Greeting:** Begin the message with a greeting which creates a friendly but business-like tone. If you know the person well, you may use their first name, e.g. **Dear Margaret** or **Hello Margaret**. If the person receiving the email is unknown to you or more senior, it is better to use the surname and title, e.g. **Dear Mr Smith, Dear Ms O'Connor**.

3. **Use concise, clear expression:** Nobody wants to wade through a long, rambling email.

4. **Purpose:** Clearly indicate what the message is about in the first paragraph. Give full details in the following paragraph(s).

5. **Action:** Any action that you want the reader to take should be clearly described, using polite phrases such as **Could you…** or **I would be grateful if …**

6. **Attachments:** Make sure you refer in the main message to any attachments you are adding.

7. **Closing message:** A brief, polite phrase will nicely round out your email, e.g. **Thank you for your time, I look forward to your response**.

8. **Conclusions:** Conclude the message politely. Common endings are **Yours sincerely, Kind regards**.

9. **Review:** Before you click 'send', take a moment to review your email. Check for grammatical or spelling errors. Typos suggest carelessness and can even convey incorrect information.

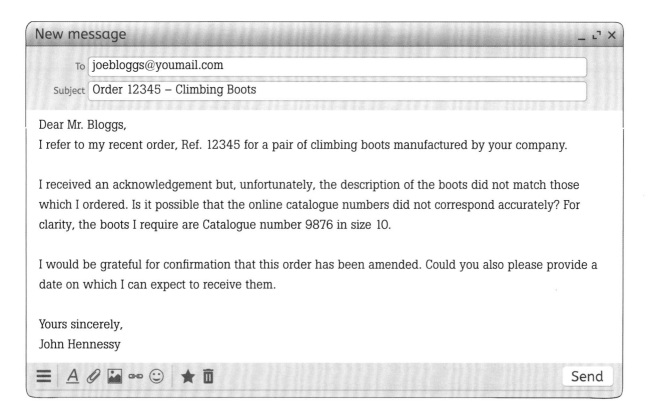

New message

To: joebloggs@youmail.com

Subject: Order 12345 – Climbing Boots

Dear Mr. Bloggs,

I refer to my recent order, Ref. 12345 for a pair of climbing boots manufactured by your company.

I received an acknowledgement but, unfortunately, the description of the boots did not match those which I ordered. Is it possible that the online catalogue numbers did not correspond accurately? For clarity, the boots I require are Catalogue number 9876 in size 10.

I would be grateful for confirmation that this order has been amended. Could you also please provide a date on which I can expect to receive them.

Yours sincerely,
John Hennessy

Send

Tasks

Practise formal letter and email writing by completing the following tasks. Make sure that you follow the guidelines for formal letters and business emails and check your work against each point.

1. Write a letter or email to the author of any text you have studied, telling him / her whether or not you enjoyed it, and explaining why.

2. You need a reference letter from your principal to secure a summer job. Write the letter you would like him/her to supply you with. (The address you use should not be that of your actual school, nor should you use your own name.)

3. An article has appeared in a daily newspaper, in print and online, claiming that 'teenagers nowadays have no moral standards'. Write a letter of reply in which you respond to this charge.

4. Write an email of complaint to a shop which sold you a defective item. Explain exactly the nature of the problem and clarify what action you expect to be taken.

5. Write an email to the Board of Management of your school objecting to the rules concerning having to wear your school uniform during state examinations.

Use the following check-list to ensure that you are writing a good formal letter or business email.

1. Have I read the question very carefully and analysed exactly what I am being asked to do? ☐

2. Have I followed the correct format for a formal letter or email? (check guidelines) ☐

3. Have I paragraphed properly? One idea or comment per paragraph. ☐

4. Have I used formal, clear English and avoided slang or colloquial expressions? ☐

5. Have I avoided using contractions? (e.g. 'it's' instead of 'it is') ☐

6. Have I used the correct complimentary close? In letters:
   'Yours sincerely' when I know name of the recipient or
   'Yours faithfully' if I do not know their name.
   In emails: 'Yours sincerely', 'Kind regards'. ☐

7. Have I signed the letter or signed off the email correctly? ☐

8. Have I checked my spelling and grammar? ☐

If you can tick each of these boxes, you should be able to write a very good formal letter or business email.

(c) Informal/personal letters or emails

Informal or personal letters and emails are usually between two people who know each other fairly well. Some, but not all, of the rules for writing a formal letter and email apply.

Guidelines for writing an informal letter or email:

1. Letters – **Your address** should be displayed in the **top right hand corner.**

2. Letters – The **date** should be displayed just **below your address on the right.** Skip a line between your address and the date. You can write the date in full or you may use an abbreviated form e.g. 1/3/19.

3. Letters – **There is no need to write the name and address of the recipient.** This is never done in informal letters to friends and relations.

4. Letters – The **salutation or greeting** should be on the left hand side of the page, as in formal letters.

5. You can address the person by their first name e.g. Hi Joe or Dear Granny, etc.

6. You should **use paragraphs correctly**, but you are not required to state the purpose of the letter or comply with the formal letter and business email conventions.

7. The language register can be chatty, colloquial and intimate. However, avoid overuse of slang and **never** use obscene language.

8. The **final paragraph** should conclude the letter or email, but it can be less formally structured.

9. The **tone** can be humorous, sarcastic, mock-serious as well as serious or sincere.

10. You may **close informally** by using such phrases as Best wishes, Hope to see you soon, Lots of love, etc.

11. **Sign your name.** Usually, your first name is all that is required, as the recipient knows you well.

12. In the final assessment, ensure that you are **writing on the topic** outlined in the question.

Tasks

1. Read the sample informal email and informal letter in response to the question: Write an email to a friend inviting them to come on a holiday with you and your family.

2. In each of the two samples, note how the points in the *Guidelines for writing an informal letter or email* have been applied.

Sample informal email

New message	_ ⌞⌝ ✕

To: martin@youmail.com

Subject: Disneyland Paris!

Hi Martin,

Great, great news! Mum and Dad have just told me that they are taking my sister Jill and me to Disneyland in Paris for the last two weeks in June - but that's not the best part of it buddy – we can each bring a friend along because the deal is for a family with four kids and we have only two. You are my choice of friend, Martin, and you'd better get your parents to let you come along.

I know you're probably thinking that Disneyland is more for little kids. We're gone a bit beyond Mickey Mouse and Donald Duck at this stage of our lives – but think PARIS – think all those gorgeous-looking French girls working in Disneyland for the summer holidays! They might join us in the evenings for a bit of craic. Some of those thrill-seeking, roller-coaster rides could be even more thrilling with a few sweet French girls screaming with excitement as we all try out the high-octane top ten! I can nearly feel the adrenaline buzz already.

I wonder will they like my freckled face and red hair. It should make a change for them anyway and as you know, I'm dangerously handsome! Pity you're so challenged in the looks department, but I'm sure we can get some poor soul to befriend you (just joking! calm down!).

Get in to your mum and dad right now Martin and ask them can you come. Promise them that you will swot your head off for the exams and get fabulous results. We'll be back by the time the results come out, so no worries on that score. I'm going to do well in French, whatever about the rest of my subjects. I'm starting tonight on the vocab and phrases and I won't stop until I'm fluent.

I expect to know soon as my mum is going to ring your mum tonight. If they refuse, act like you're having a nervous breakdown, refuse to eat, don't wash, mope around and fight with your sister and that awful brother of yours. They'll crack and let you come with us - just for a few weeks of release from your rotten presence!

Au revoir, mon ami!

Jack

Send

Although this student has taken a light-hearted approach to the subject, all the **correct conventions** for informal letters or emails are present. The **tone is suitable** for a personal email and **reveals the character of the writer**.

Now look at a different approach to the same question:

Sample informal letter

64 Fernview Park,
Ballybeg,
Co. Donegal

23rd May 2020

Dear Anne,

It feels so long since we last met, or even wrote to each other. How are you and all your family? We are all fine here in Donegal and send good wishes to your parents and brother.

The weather has been dreadful for the last few months. We hardly saw the face of the sun for more than a few hours this month and it's the first month of summer. However, that's all about to change I hope.

My parents are bringing us to Portugal for a family holiday in July and the best part of it is that they are allowing me to bring a friend along. Brian is outgoing and makes friends easily but I'm less confident and often end up hanging around with my parents all day. It's so boring!

I would just love it if you would come along with us on this holiday Anne. We could do so many fun things together. There is a fabulous beach near our apartment and we also have our own swimming pool. It's not very big, but it is wonderful to cool down in when the sun is scorching. We are quite near to an old village which has some lovely little shops and boutiques and the clothes are quite cheap. I know you love clothes! In addition, we can go for long walks, chat, listen to music and catch up on the gossip. There are a few activities for teenagers in the next resort, but I know you're a bit like me when it comes to deafening disco music and non-stop guzzling of junk food. It's just awful. Most of those teenagers are just acting a part and following the crowd I think.

Please ask your parents if they will allow you to join us. We're going from the 10th to the 24th July. My parents will pay for the tickets etc. All you need to do is pack and make sure you bring enough money to shop in the boutiques.

I am looking forward to hearing from you soon. Please come.

Love,

Jennifer

The **tone here is quite different** from the previous sample but it **addresses the task** set in the question. The **language** here is more restrained and is effective in conveying the quiet, refined but slightly judgemental writer. One gets the sense that she is pleading for company and is a lonely kind of person. All standard letter writing conventions are observed.

Tasks

T

Tip:
A good personal letter or email will always reveal something of the character or personality of the writer and their relationship with the recipient, unlike a formal letter which is more business-like and detached in approach.

Imagine that you are Anne. Write a response to Jennifer's letter.

2. Reports

Reports are written for several reasons:

- To **communicate** ideas, information, facts and findings in a **logical** manner.
- To **research** some issue or problem and come to conclusions based on this research.
- To **make recommendations** for improvements or for advisable changes.
- To **record** information for various purposes.

Format for Reports:

The format for any report is related to the type of report that is being written. A police report, following a road accident, would be quite different from a report which researches some issue or problem in order to make recommendations for change or improvements. Similarly, a newspaper report on some matter of public interest, has its own structure and conventions which differ from other types of report writing. In other words, there is no 'one size fits all' formula for writing reports.

Guidelines for writing a report:

- You must be conscious of the reader and write in a formal, clear and simple style.
- Unless your readers are experts on the subject of the report, avoid all use of jargon or technical terms which could confuse them.
- Write in a structured format using any technique which communicates the information clearly and efficiently.
- Reports should **not** be written in the first person (i.e. 'I'). Using 'I' can make the content sound less objective.
- Good spelling, punctuation and grammar are essential in report writing.

In this section, guidelines for four report styles are provided. These styles are:
(a) Report based on research or a survey
(b) Report based on an eyewitness account
(c) Report to be published in a school magazine or on a school website
(d) News reports

(a) Report based on research or a survey

Format for reports based on research or a survey:

This type of report requires:
- A clear **layout**.
- A **title** which indicates the issue being researched and reported on.
- A **date**.
- The **name of the author or authors**.
- The **name/s of the person, people or group who commissioned the report**.

Guidelines for writing a report based on research or a survey:

Step 1

Before you begin, ask yourself the following questions:
- **Who** requested the report and **why** did they request it?
- What is **the purpose** of this report?
- **Who engaged in the research** and **what methods were used**?

The answers to these questions will provide you with the **Terms of Reference** for the report and they will help you to decide how you should gather information for your report (the **Procedure**).

Step 2

The next step is to **plan** the report.
- Begin by deciding on **an appropriate title** as this ensures a sharp focus.
- Decide on what **information, facts, evidence** etc. are relevant and essential. **Be selective** as the report must be **concise and clear**.
- **Organise** your material into a **logical** sequence.
- Before you begin writing:
  - decide what you learnt from your research
  - draw logical conclusions from this
  - decide what recommendations to make.

Step 3

The next step is to **write** the report.
- Maintain an **objective** approach.
- **Present the report in a visually pleasing way.** Use headings, sub-headings (if necessary), bullet-pointed lists and allow plenty of 'white space'. It can be very off-putting to see large chunks of printed text.
- Check **grammar, punctuation and spelling**.
- **Sign** the report.

Sample Report based on research or a survey

You have been asked by the Board of Management of your school to investigate the canteen facilities for students in the school and to make recommendations for improvements based on your findings.
Write the report which you would submit.

Report on Canteen Facilities at St. Brigid's College, Wexford

Terms of Reference:

This report was commissioned by the Board of Management, St. Brigid's College, Wexford in order to evaluate the canteen facilities in the school and to make recommendations for improvements based on the findings.

Procedure:

The researchers interviewed a cross-section of twenty students from each of the six year groups in the school, making a total of 120 students, and asked them the following questions:

Food:
1. How would you describe the quality and choice of food offered in the canteen?
2. Do you consider that the food is good value for money?
(Note: Students were asked to respond using the words Poor, Good or Excellent.)

Environment:
3. What aspect of the canteen environment most needs improvement?

Findings:
1. In answer to the question of quality and choice of food:
    - 91 described it as Poor.
    - 25 described it as Good.
    - 4 described it as Excellent.
2. In answer to the question of value for money:
    - 93 considered it Poor.
    - 23 considered it Good.
    - 4 considered it Excellent.
3. As regards the aspect of the environment which most needs improvement:
    - 75 referred to the lack of adequate space in the canteen.
    - 25 referred to the dark decor and peeling paintwork.
    - 20 referred to the inadequate maintenance of proper order when queuing.

Conclusions:
1. The quality and choice of food on offer in the canteen is generally unsatisfactory and needs to be reviewed.
2. The price of the food on offer needs to be revised as it exceeds the value to be had elsewhere.
3. The lack of sufficient space in the canteen needs to be addressed and the decor needs upgrading.

Recommendations:
1. Students should be offered a wider variety of nutritious options. While some students enjoy fried foods such as burgers and chips, others would prefer grilled or baked hot dishes and some vegetarian choices. Salads would be a welcome addition.
2. The company which runs the canteen should lower prices in keeping with the value offered in the local garage shops and supermarkets. If the present caterers resist lowering prices, then the contract should be offered to another, more competitive company.
3. As the canteen becomes over-crowded, consideration should be given to the possibility of staggering lunch times for seniors and juniors. As school numbers are growing, a new, larger canteen will need to be built eventually.
4. The canteen urgently needs to be painted. We suggest that this is a project which Transition Year students could undertake with appropriate supervision.
5. More adult supervision is needed to ensure orderly queuing.

Report compiled and signed by:
Gillian Adams • Anthony Burke • Michael King • Rosemary Murphy.

All of the above students are members of the School Student Committee.
Date: 18th September 2017.

Tasks

1. Read the guidelines on page 139 for writing a report based on research or a survey. Does the report on page 140 conform to those guidelines?

2. A report can also be presented as an info-graphic. Study the infographic below on new-age media carefully then complete the following sentences using only information provided.

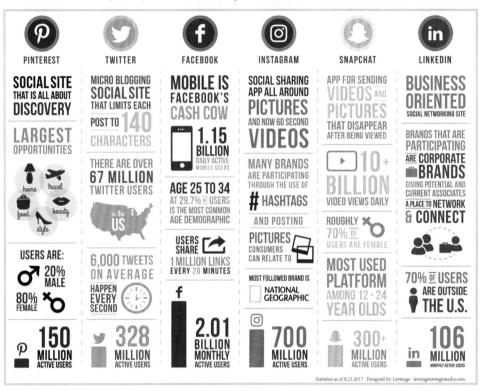

Statistics as of 8.25.2017 Designed by: Leverage - leveragenewagemedia.com

   (a)   The most popular form of social media is _____
   (b)   The most common age demographic for Facebook is

   _____
   (c)   The percentage of Linkedin users living inside the United States
         is _____
   (d)   One major difference between Instagram and Snapchat is

   _____
   (e)   The platform most used by teenagers is _____
   (f)   The purpose of Linkedin is   _____

   _____
   (g)   I think that Pinterest is more appealing to women because

   _____
   _____

3. Which of the two reports A (Canteen facilities) or B (Info-graphic on new-age media) do you find most effective at conveying information? Explain your response.

(b) Report based on an eyewitness account

Sample eyewitness report

You have witnessed a serious fight which took place on the school premises. The principal of your school is compiling a report for the Board of Management, which will also be given to the parents of the students involved. You have been asked by the principal to write an eyewitness report of what you saw and heard. Write the text of your report.

Fight in Students' Locker Room

On Wednesday, the 24th March at approximately 2.00.p.m, I was in the Junior students' locker room, collecting my books for the afternoon classes.

As I was closing my locker door, I heard somebody shouting outside the door of the room and another person shouting back at them.

A group of students suddenly entered the room and I noticed that one of the boys, Michael Aherne, was holding an open pen-knife in his hand and pointing it at John Roche, who was holding a hurley. Other students who were present included Alan Casey, Niall Corbett and Peter Lynch.

Niall Corbett tried to intervene but was threatened with a blow from the hurley held by John Roche.

I tried to exit the room but could not do so because the door was being blocked by Michael Aherne. Both boys were shouting loudly and threatening to kill each other.

John Roche knocked the pen-knife out of Michael Aherne's hand with the hurley, but Michael Aherne managed to retrieve it and they both began to physically attack each other. I saw blood pouring from the side of John Roche's face and observed him swinging the hurley, which hit Michael Aherne's head. Alan and Niall tried to break the fight up, while Peter managed to exit the room and ran to call a teacher.

Within minutes, two teachers, Mr O'Connor and Mr Murphy, arrived. They attempted to break up the fight but both boys continued until Mr Murphy grabbed the hurley from John Roche's hand. John Roche was bleeding badly at this stage. Michael Aherne then threw the pen-knife to the ground and sat on one of the benches with his head leaning against the wall.

Mr O'Connor noticed me and asked me if I had witnessed the entire fight. I told him that I had only witnessed what had taken place in the locker room. He asked me to accompany him to the principal's office. As I left the locker room, Mr Murphy was phoning for an ambulance, while Alan Casey and Peter Lynch were talking quietly to Michael Aherne. Two other teachers, Ms O'Brien and Mr Burke arrived in the locker room just as I was leaving with Mr O'Connor.

Signed: Patrick Foley

You will notice that the writer of this eyewitness has:
- given a logical account of the fight which he witnessed.
- not used any exaggeration or dramatic expressions.
- not offered any opinion on who was to blame for the fight.
- named other witnesses to the fight.
- only referred to his own situation in order to explain why he did not leave the room.
- written in clear, simple language.

Tasks

Imagine that you are Patrick Foley. Write your diary entry for the day you witnessed the fight in the locker room. Remember that a diary entry refers to the facts but is also personal and reflects your own feelings and opinions about the event.

(c) Report to be published in a school magazine or website

Sample report on a school trip

SCHOOL TIMES

| NEWS | SPORT | LEARNING | ABOUT | EVENTS | GALLERY |

Extra-curricular | School trips

Ski Trip to Austria 2020

Every year, students eagerly anticipate the school ski trip to Austria, and this year did not disappoint our high expectations.

On 27ᵗʰ March, we travelled by air and coach until we reached the beautiful little village of Itter, set in the Austrian Tyrol. You can read all about this wonderful village at https://www.tyrol.com. Some sunny weather had melted the snow on the lower slopes. However, most of us had some previous experience of skiing, so we were able to go further up the mountains where the air was deep and thick.

Our instructors were really fantastic. The fact that our only injuries were a few bumps and bruises speaks volumes for the expert tuition we received. Ms Cotter, armed with her first-aid kit, was able to deal with every situation that arose and, thankfully, we did not need to visit the local hospital.

Evening activities were varied and extremely enjoyable. We had lots of fun playing competitive games against the teachers - especially when we beat them more often than not!

Our reluctance to leave Itter and journey home was only relieved by the day we spent shopping in Munich, which is a truly beautiful city.

We are all grateful to the teachers who organised and accompanied us on the trip. They do every year in order to allow us to have such a wonderful and educational experience.

Thanks are also due to our drivers, Bill and Tom, who tolerated our raucous singing. Their good humour and patience added to the success of the whole trip.

We all have happy memories from our week in Austria and hope next year's group have as good a time as we did.

To see some photos of our trip, click on the 'Gallery 2' link below.

Tasks

(a) Identify two digital elements used in the report on page 143.

(b) How can the use of digital elements, like the ones you have identified above, lead to more effective communication? You may refer to this report or any other reports, articles or blogs in your answer.

(c) How is this type of report different from the info-graphic on new-age media on page 141?

(d) News reports

A news report informs readers of **the facts surrounding various events** and who or what may be affected by these events. The two most important elements of a news report are **facts** and **style**.

Facts:

- The facts of any given news event can be gained quickly by asking the **5 'W' questions** 'who, what, when, where, why'.
- Writers must ensure that the facts they report on are **accurate**.
- **Avoid sensationalism**, such as appears in tabloid journalism.
- News reports **deal with the truth** and **should not contain any bias or personal opinion**.

Style:

- The style of a report should be **direct and concise**.
- Avoid using **unnecessary words** or engaging in **lengthy description**.
- Use **clear expression** which communicates with a **general readership**. A news report is not the place to try and impress people with your command of language. **So keep vocabulary simple**.
- **Verbs should be active rather than passive** e.g. '*The boy kicked the ball through the window*' rather than '*The ball was kicked through the window by the boy*'.
- Paragraphs should be kept **short** and contain **one main point**.

Most Newsworthy Info
Who? What? When? Where? Why? How?

Important Details

Other General Info

Background Info

News reports usually employ the classic inverted pyramid where all of the 5 'W' questions are answered first. This is followed by further important details and concludes with background information or other material which could be omitted without affecting the facts on which the report is based. Editors can print the entire story or easily cut from the bottom section.

Unit 4: Literacy

Sample News Report

Garda 'bait bikes' plan to swoop on thieves leads to arrests in capital
Cormac McQuinn

A Garda operation involving so-called 'bait bikes' to lure would-be thieves has led to 16 arrests in the capital, new figures reveal.

Bikes were deliberately left in 'hot spot' locations in the south city on 50 occasions under Operation Chain, with gardaí monitoring them, ready to swoop if anyone attempted to make off with

them. New figures provided to Social Democrats TD Róisín Shortall suggest that arrests were made in around a third of instances that 'bait bikes' were deployed.

Now Ms Shortall has suggested the operation could be expanded to university campuses and to cities like Cork and Galway, on a pilot basis. The Dublin north-west TD said: "Bike theft is a real problem for cyclists in Dublin city and other cities and yet, because it often goes unreported to gardaí, it's difficult to get a proper sense of the scale of it.

"Gardaí's novel use of decoy bikes as a type of honey trap for thieves could be a useful deterrent," she added.

She said that any such operation should be justified by a "high rate of arrests and the appropriate number of prosecutions". Ms Shortall stressed that prevention is "always better than cure" and noted the need for bike users to have good locks.

She also said offices, apartment blocks and third-level institutions should have proper facilities where people can park their bikes so they are not left on the streets.

Operation Chain was devised by local Garda management in the Pearse Street Garda District.

In the information provided to Ms Shortall, Justice Minister Charlie Flanagan outlined how it is an intelligence-led operation and involves co-operation with Dublin City Council.

Gardaí have a number of 'bait bikes' that are deployed at 'hot spot' locations by the community policing unit.

The bikes are kept under surveillance by gardaí who intercept individuals attempting to steal them. There are also follow-up enquiries with online retailers to see if the individual has been involved in attempts to sell bikes through websites.

The 16 arrests occurred in the year up to March. Of those cases, seven have been finalised with outcomes including three offenders receiving the Probation Act, one person sentenced to community service and another receiving an adult caution. Six other cases are before the courts.

Irish Independent
IRELAND'S BEST-SELLING DAILY NEWSPAPER

Questions

1. Explain each of the following words as used in the article:
   (a) deployed
   (b) expanded
   (c) deterrent
   (d) devised
   (e) surveillance
   (f) intercept

2. What is your understanding of each of the following words and phrases as used in the article:
   (a) bait-bikes
   (b) to lure would-be thieves
   (c) a type of honey trap
   (d) intelligence-led operation

Tip:
An effective news report will have a strong 'lead' or opening sentence in order to grab the attention of the reader. In the above sample, the first sentence encourages the reader to read on.

Tasks

1. Imagine you are a writer with your school magazine or website. Write a report of a recent sports event involving your school team. Try to capture the atmosphere of the event for your readers.

2. The Transition Year class in your school carried out a survey of how many students in their year group use social media and their attitudes to the time spent on social media. Based on the data supplied below, write a report on this survey for your school magazine or website.

Social media use	Males	Females
Percentage with a social media account.	97%	98%
Percentage with multiple social media accounts.	90%	97%
Percentage who believe they are addicted to social media.	43%	41%
Percentage using social media more than two hours a day.	94%	96%
Percentage who play a musical instrument or read for pleasure.	18%	21%
Percentage who regularly engage in sports.	73%	69%

3. You witnessed a traffic accident on your way to school and have been asked to write a report on it for the Garda Síochána. Write the report you would submit.

4. Imagine you are a journalist with a local newspaper. Write a short report on a criminal offence which was committed in your neighbourhood.

Use the following checklist to ensure that you are writing a good report:

1. Have I read the question very carefully and analysed exactly what I am being asked to do? ☐
2. Have I followed the correct format for the report? (check guidelines) ☐
3. Have I paragraphed properly? One idea or comment per paragraph. ☐
4. Have I maintained objectivity and avoided bias? ☐
5. Have I used formal, clear English and avoided slang or colloquial expressions? ☐
6. Have I avoided using contractions? (e.g. 'I've' instead of 'I have'). ☐
7. Have I signed the report correctly? ☐
8. Have I checked my spelling and grammar? ☐

If you can tick each of these boxes, you should be able to write very good reports.

3. Reviews

A review is an individual response to a book, film, event, etc. The reviewer expresses his/her judgement to the work presented. A review is, therefore, subjective. Different reviewers may respond differently to the same book, film, event.

In this section guidelines for two types of review are provided. These are:

(a) Book reviews

(b) Film reviews

(a) Book reviews

Guidelines for writing a book review:

- **Brainstorm and plan** your ideas before you begin writing.
- **State the title of the book** and **the name of the author** in the first paragraph.
- **What is the genre of the book:** science fiction, thriller, mystery, adventure?
- **Give a brief outline of the setting and plot** – but do not write a summary and never tell how it ends.
- **Describe the main characters.** Are they realistic or stereotypes? What is their importance to the story?
- **Comment on the major themes.** What sort of ideas and issues does the story deal with? What does the book make you think about?
- **Comment on style.** Is the story written in the first or third person? ('I' or 'he/she') How did this affect the story? Comment on the atmosphere and the author's use of language, dialogue and imagery. Is the setting described in detail? Are emotions and attitudes described in depth?
- **Personal Response.** Think about **why** you enjoyed or did not enjoy the book. Did it affect you in any way? Could you identify with any of the characters and the situations in which they found themselves? Have you learned anything from the book (e.g. about yourself, other people, life in general)?
- Give the book a **rating**, e.g. 4/5, three out of four stars etc.

Recommendation.

– Audience.

– Comparison

Sample book review

The book which I am reviewing is *The Boy in the Striped Pyjamas* by **John Boyne**. It is a fictional story set during the time of the Holocaust.

When Bruno, the main character, is forced to move away from his Berlin home with his family, his life changes forever. His beautiful home in Germany is replaced by a much smaller, duller house, which is also the location of his father's downstairs office. His father does not explain or discuss his occupation with his children. However, the reader soon realises that Bruno's father is a Nazi Commandant in Auschwitz.

Despite the setting, the reader is spared many of the horrific details of what actually took place in the concentration camp itself. This, I believe, increases the shock when we discover exactly what is going on there.

The Boy in the Striped Pyjamas

JOHN BOYNE

I found the book intriguing and a real page-turner. However, it was difficult to fully believe that a nine-year-old, intelligent boy like Bruno could really be so naïve as to think that all the people were wearing pyjamas instead of prison uniforms. It was also very difficult to believe that Bruno and Schmuel, a young prisoner whom he befriends, could meet, have conversations and play games without being noticed by anybody. The adult characters were far more credible and created a major contrast to the two boys.

The style of the writing is clear and straightforward because it explores and captures the mind of a child. The deliberate mistakes of 'Fury' for Führer, and 'Out-With' for Auschwitz are funny in a dark sort of way and made me feel a strong sense of foreboding right from the start.

Although the book is easy to read, it deals with some very serious themes and issues which I found disturbing.

I would consider this book unsuitable for any reader under the age of eleven or twelve. It is, however, a very good, thought-provoking read for teenagers.

I would recommend it and would give it a rating of 9 / 10

Tasks

The writer of this review considers the novel, *The Boy in the Striped Pyjamas*, unsuitable for readers under the age of eleven or twelve. Based on the review, suggest three reasons why the writer may think that.

(b) Film Reviews

Guidelines for writing a film review:

The guidelines for writing a film review are similar to those for writing a book review. The major differences are:

- Instead of referring to the author, you refer to the director of the film.
- You name the lead actors who play the different characters in the film.
- You could refer to costuming, makeup, set-design, music, special effects etc.

Sample film review

Tasks

1. This review is based on the novel which was reviewed on page 148. Compare the film and book reviews and make a list of the differences.

> **The Boy in the Striped Pyjamas**, directed by Mark Herman, offers us a fresh look at the horrific atrocities of the Holocaust. In just 90 minutes, it manages to create heart-breaking poignancy similar to that of 'Schindler's List' or 'The Diary of Anne Frank'.
>
> Bruno, played by Asa Butterfield, is a German 9-year old. His father (David Thewliss) is an SS officer who runs a concentration camp. The drama unfolds through the boy's innocent, confused eyes. Part of the power of the film is due to the fact that we, the audience, know what is going on whereas Bruno does not. We understand the significance of the death's head on the collar tab which his father wears.
>
> The city setting in Berlin, where Bruno plays happily with his friends, is captured well in the opening sequences but the location changes dramatically when the family move to the countryside near Auschwitz. Bruno, who thinks the place is called 'Out-With', can see what he thinks is a farm from a window that his mother (Vera Farmiga) has sealed. He can see what he believes are the 'striped pyjamas' of the inmates - pyjamas similar to those worn by Pavel (David Hayman), the frail old man who works in their garden.
>
> Loneliness and curiosity drive Bruno to explore beyond the bounds of his garden fence. He discovers a quiet, unguarded area of the fence where he meets Shmuel (Jack Scanlon), a boy his own age who is equally confused by the events taking place around him.
>
> Mark Herman directs the film using a simple, uncluttered style which heightens the profound impact on the viewer. He allows us to see the horror of the Holocaust through the unknowing eyes of a child. We see Bruno peeping in the door as his father and other soldiers watch a Nazi propaganda film about the camp. We sense his fear of the brutal staff officer (Rupert Friend) who describes Jews as being 'evil' and we can almost smell the smoke which Bruno sees curling from the chimneys in the death camp.
>
> The film focuses on complex emotional issues of evil and the Holocaust, and raises questions about the nature of man. I found it disturbing but deeply thought-provoking.
>
> I would highly recommend **The Boy in the Striped Pyjamas** to anybody over the age of 13.
>
> My rating is 5 out of 5 stars.

2. Write a critical analysis of the poster for the film, *'The Boy in the Striped Pyjamas'*. In it you should consider:
   (a) The visual impact of the poster.
   (b) Whether or not the poster makes you want to see the film.
3. Having read both the book and film reviews, suggest a different design for a poster for the film. In it you should concentrate on the illustration, wording of any accompanying text and the use of colour and light to capture mood.

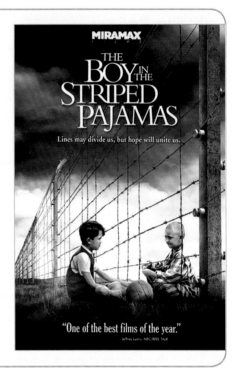

4. Blogs

A blog is a regularly updated personal website or online diary on which you can record your opinions, offer information, display photographs, video clips or other visual material and offer links to other sites etc.

The purpose of a blog depends on the kind of blog it is, e.g. a travel blog, a film review blog, a cookery blog, a personal diary concerning some major event etc.

You need to be able to write and structure your blog in a way that makes it accessible and relevant to your readers.

Blog structure:

- Blog entries are posted in reverse-chronological order, running from the most recent to the least recent. The date and the time posted are included with the name of the blogger. Alternatively, the blogger might end the post with 'Posted by [blogger's name]'.
- Create a **title** that will appeal to your reader. The title helps your reader decide if the blog is something they are interested in. Remember that your readers are really anyone interested in your topic.
- Write the **main point** in the opening paragraph. This gives a sharp focus to your blog and encourages the reader to continue reading.
- You can elaborate in the other paragraphs of your post.
- Readers and the blogger can usually **comment** on (or reply to) a blog entry. The comments can turn into a dialogue, with the readers and blogger talking together.

Blog writing style:

- Keep your style chatty and informal. Use first person 'I' and be honest and forthright in your views. Keep your readers in mind and try to maintain their interest in your topic.
- Use short, precise sentences with single ideas. There's nothing more boring than repetition, so vary your word choices to keep your writing fresh.
- Keep to the point and stay within the realms of your blog's main area.

Blog topics:

- It is always best to write about something you are personally interested in and are enthusiastic about.
- You could write about some new experience, any ideas you gained, any problems you encountered and how you resolved them.
- You could recommend articles on websites that you have read or found useful.
- Blogs often use pictures, photographs, short videos, links, etc. which attract readers and add interest.

Sample blog

20th April 2020

Skeletons in the Cupboard

Hi everyone!

If there's one thing I absolutely love doing in my spare time it's researching the history of my ancestors and finding out more about the characters with whom I share my DNA.

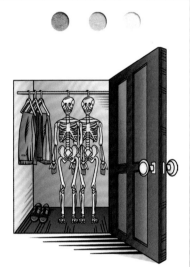

Lots of people would find this a very boring topic but it's actually really fascinating.
What started off as a hobby last year, has now become a passion and I absolutely enjoy every minute of it.

Not everyone in my family is happy about my ancestor-hunting, however. My grandfather was particularly reluctant and tried to talk me into, what he considered, more interesting projects such as writing film reviews or perhaps a travel blog about family holidays over the years.

I was surprised by his sudden interest in keeping me away from too much knowledge of my family roots but all has become clear to me now. I found a skeleton in our family closet! It was my great-great-grandfather, Jack Matthews, who was jailed in 1881 for taking part in a public brawl on the streets of Dublin. Jack, it seems, had very strong political views which were very different from those of his neighbours. During a particularly heated argument with a group of 'Jackeens' as he called them, he lost all control of his temper and lashed out with his fists, breaking the nose of one man and giving a black eye to another. The fact that he had just spent a few hours drinking beforehand didn't help matters. Anyway, he was hauled before the magistrates and spent twelve months calming down in prison.

How do I know all this? I was able to read all about it in the 'Dublin Gazette', a popular newspaper at that time. Of course, I wouldn't have known anything at all if I hadn't been researching my family roots. One thing leads to another when you start doing that and I suppose I got lucky and discovered a family secret that was kept well-hidden for a few generations. Now I know where I got my hot temper from!

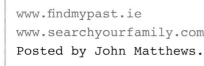

Check back in over the next few weeks and I'll let you know some very interesting stuff about my grand-aunt on my mother's side. This is her photograph:

Believe me, she is worth hearing about too - much to my mum's dismay!

If you're interested in finding out more about how you could trace some of your own ancestors, click on one of the links below and get started.

www.findmypast.ie
www.searchyourfamily.com
Posted by John Matthews.

Comments

petersullivan: I checked out that link and you're right. This could get really interesting.

mikekearney: Even when he was out of his mind on drink? Get real!

johnmatthews: He doesn't follow my blog so he won't see it. By the way, I'm not ashamed of my ancestor. I think he was a man who knew his own mind.

joebloggs: Do you really think it's okay to share private family info on a blog like this? Have you considered the feelings of your grandfather?

Tasks

Write a blog post on a topic that you are really interested in. Follow the guidelines on page 150.

5. Blurbs

A blurb is a short description of a book, written on the back page. It is intended to **encourage a person to read the book**. Blurbs do not have to follow any particular formats, but you should be aware of basic guidelines.

Guidelines for writing a blurb:

- Blurbs should be concise and simply written. Keep sentences short.
- You should use persuasive techniques to encourage the reader to read the book.
- What is left unsaid can be just as important as what is said and can create a sense of mystery to 'hook' the reader.
- Never give any clues as to how the book will end.

> **Tip:**
> The following blurb is taken from the website goodreads.com. You you can find plenty of similar examples on the internet, or just look at the blurbs on the books in your school library.

Sample blurb 1

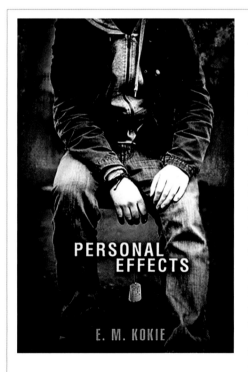

Personal Effects
by E.M. Kokie

After his older brother dies in Iraq, Matt makes a discovery that rocks his beliefs about strength, bravery, and honour in this page-turning debut.

Ever since his brother, T.J., was killed in Iraq, Matt feels like he's been sleepwalking through life - failing classes, getting into fights, and avoiding his dad's lectures about following in his brother's footsteps. T.J.'s gone, but Matt can't shake the feeling that if only he could get his hands on his brother's stuff from Iraq, he'd be able to make sense of his death. However, as Matt searches for answers about T.J.'s death, he faces a shocking revelation about T.J.'s life that suggests he may not have known T.J. as well as he thought. What he learns challenges him to stand up to his father, honour his brother's memory, and take charge of his own life. With compassion, humour, and a compelling narrative voice, E. M. Kokie explores grief, social mores, and self-discovery in a provocative first novel.

This next blurb is the text from the back of the book *The Boy in the Striped Pyjamas.*

Sample blurb 2

The Boy in the Striped Pyjamas
by John Boyne

The story of *The Boy in the Striped Pyjamas* is very difficult to describe. Usually we give some clues about the book on the cover, but in this case we think that would spoil the reading of the book. We think it is important that you start to read without knowing what it is about. If you do start to read this book, you will go on a journey with a nine-year-old boy called Bruno. (Though this isn't a book for nine-year-olds.) Sooner or later you will arrive with Bruno at a fence. We hope you never have to cross such a fence.

Tasks

(a) Compare the two sample blurbs. Which is more effective in your opinion? Give reasons for your answer.

(b) How does each blurb correspond to the guidelines already outlined on page 153?

(c) Write a blurb for a book you have read.

B. Oral Literacy

1. Oral language

Oral language is the system through which we use spoken words to express knowledge, ideas, and feelings. Oral literacy requires a clear sense of genre, audience, purpose and style.

> **Tip:**
> Remember GAPS – Genre, Audience, Purpose, Style

Listeners differ from readers in that they only <u>hear</u> the words spoken and <u>observe</u> the delivery of such words.

- **Language should be clear** and word choice appropriate for the specific audience.
- Sentences should be concise and varied but **never rambling** or the listener will get confused.
- The speaker must have a clear sense of the **purpose** of what they are saying.
- They must have an awareness of their **audience**. The **register** or appropriateness of the style of text must suit the audience.
- Speakers who are passionate about what they are saying tend to use their entire bodies to support the message they wish to convey. **Tone**, **gestures**, **pace** and **pause** all combine in the effective delivery of the content.
- Much of the impact of oral language depends upon **body language** which comprises **gesture**, **stance**, and **facial expression**.
    - (i) **Gestures** can be used to emphasise a point, to indicate someone or something nearby or to express an emotion. Most people naturally use such gestures when they are engaged in lively discussion - pointing, throwing hands in the air, shrugging shoulders, nodding head etc. It comes naturally!
    - (ii) **Stance** refers to the way someone stands or moves while speaking. Confident speakers stand on both feet and lean slightly toward the audience. This creates the impression of getting closer to their listeners. Walking around can sometimes be effective but needs to be punctuated with periods of stillness. Constant walking or swaying, creates distraction and can annoy your listeners.
    - (iii) **Facial expression** is another key aspect of effective oral communication. Eye contact is the most important element in showing your credibility and sincerity whether in a large or a small group. Good speakers engage one person at a time and use **pauses** to allow a point to sink in.
- **Pauses** are particularly effective after rhetorical questions. By using such pauses, they engage the attention of the entire audience.
- The **pace** or speed of the delivery is also very important. Too slow creates boredom; too quick creates confusion. The most effective presentations vary pace to suit what is being said.

As a listener, you need to listen **actively**, not passively. By being aware of the style, structure, content and delivery of an oral text, you maximise your understanding of oral literacy skills and become a better communicator yourself in the process.

Tasks

1. Work in pairs and take turns practising the extract from this speech out loud. Discuss how the pauses and change of pace add to the impact of the words spoken.

'I have cherished the ideal *(pause)* of a democratic and free society *(pause, then getting louder)* in which *(sweeping hand gesture indicating entire courtroom)* all persons live together in harmony and with equal opportunities. *(pause)* It is an ideal, which I hope to live for and to achieve. *(pause)* But if needs be, *(slower, quieter but with emphasis)* it is an ideal for which I am prepared to die.'

Nelson Mandela

2. (i) Read the following short extract from a TED Talk and insert, in brackets, appropriate directions for an effective oral presentation.

'When I was in the fifth grade, I bought an issue of "DC Comics Presents #57" off a spinner rack at my local bookstore, and that comic book changed my life. The combination of words and pictures did something inside my head that had never been done before, and I immediately fell in love with the medium of comics. I became a voracious comic book reader, but I never brought them to school. Instinctively, I knew that comic books didn't belong in the classroom. My parents definitely were not fans, and I was certain that my teachers wouldn't be either. After all, they never used them to teach. Comic books and graphic novels were never allowed during silent sustained reading, and they were never sold at our annual book fair. Even so, I kept reading comics, and I even started making them. Eventually I became a published cartoonist, writing and drawing comic books for a living.'

Gene Luen Yang 'Comics belong in the classroom' at TEDx ManhattanBeach

(ii) If possible, listen to the TED Talk and compare the directions you gave, with how Gene Luen Yang delivered the speech.

3. Read the following short extract from a speech by President Michael D. Higgins and insert, in brackets, appropriate directions for an effective oral presentation.

> 'All of our athletes here today are citizens we can be very proud of indeed. You are citizens who have refused to be defined or limited by the narrow stereotypes that still linger in our society today. Instead you have embraced the expectation that you too can succeed; can aspire to live the life of your choice; have your voices heard; your talents respected; and can and should be defined by your skills and abilities and by all of your possibilities.'

4. (i) Read the following extract from a TED Talk by Lisa Feldman Barrett, 'You aren't at the mercy of your emotions – your brain creates them'. Insert, in brackets, appropriate directions for an effective oral presentation.

TED Ideas worth spreading   WATCH   DISCOVER   ATTEND   PARTICIPATE   ABOUT   LOG IN

So what are emotions really? Well, strap on your seat belt, because ... emotions are guesses. They are guesses that your brain constructs in the moment where billions of brain cells are working together, and you have more control over those guesses than you might imagine that you do. Now, if that sounds preposterous to you, or, you know, kind of crazy, I'm right there with you, because frankly, if I hadn't seen the evidence for myself, decades of evidence for myself, I am fairly sure that I wouldn't believe it either. But the bottom line is that emotions are not built into your brain at birth. They are just built.

Lisa Feldman Barrett at TED@IBM

(ii) If possible, listen to the TED Talk and compare the directions you gave, with how Lisa Feldman Barrett delivered the speech.

For each of the extracts 1-4, select the best word to describe the appropriate tone. Explain your choice.
1. (a) excited (b) solemn (c) casual (d) sarcastic
2. (a) chatty (b) serious (c) excited (d) formal
3. (a) solemn (b) chatty (c) celebratory (d) informal
4. (a) celebratory (b) formal (c) informal (d) sombre

"Any given Sunday" speech

2. Questions on Oral Literacy

Speech 1

This speech, 'Ain't I a Woman?', was delivered by Sojourner Truth to a live audience in December 1851 at the Women's Convention, Akron, Ohio. Sojourner Truth was a nineteenth-century African-American woman who sought women's rights and the abolition of slavery. A charismatic speaker, she became one of the best-known abolitionists of her day. Born a slave, she was freed in 1828 when a New York law abolished slavery within the state.

Her most famous speech, 'Ain't I a Woman?' challenged cultural beliefs, including the natural inferiority of women, and biblical justifications for the second-class status of women.

Before her speech, male speakers had argued in favour of men's superior rights and privileges on the grounds of their superior intellect and the manhood of Christ. As the convention was heating up, the dignified Sojourner Truth—who was in her 60s at the time—rose slowly from her seat in a corner of the room. Amid shouts of 'Don't let her speak!' and hissing, she moved to the front, laid her bonnet down, and began her speech.

Unit 4: Literacy

'Well, children, where there is so much racket there must be something out of kilter. I think that 'twixt the negroes of the South and the women at the North, all talking about rights, the white men will be in a fix pretty soon. But what's all this here talking about?

That man over there says that women need to be helped into carriages, and lifted over ditches, and to have the best place everywhere. Nobody ever helps me into carriages, or over mud-puddles, or gives me any best place! And ain't I a woman? Look at me! Look at my arm! I have ploughed and planted, and gathered into barns, and no man could head me! And ain't I a woman? I could work as much and eat as much as a man - when I could get it - and bear the lash as well! And ain't I a woman? I have borne thirteen children, and seen most all sold off to slavery, and when I cried out with my mother's grief, none but Jesus heard me! And ain't I a woman?

Then they talk about this thing in the head; what's this they call it? [member of audience whispers, "intellect"] That's it, honey. What's that got to do with women's rights or negroes' rights? If my cup won't hold but a pint, and yours holds a quart, wouldn't you be mean not to let me have my little half measure full?

Then that little man in black there, he says women can't have as much rights as men, 'cause Christ wasn't a woman! Where did your Christ come from? From God and a woman! Man had nothing to do with Him.

If the first woman God ever made was strong enough to turn the world upside down all alone, these women together ought to be able to turn it back, and get it right side up again! And now they is asking to do it, the men better let them.

Obliged to you for hearing me, and now old Sojourner ain't got nothing more to say.'

Questions

1. In your view, what elements of the speech would have made it engaging for the audience? Explain your answer by referring to both the style and the content of the speech.

2. What tone of voice would be appropriate for each of these statements from the speech? Explain your responses.

   (i) 'Look at me! Look at my arm! I have ploughed and planted, and gathered into barns, and no man could head me! And ain't I a woman?'

   (ii) 'I have borne thirteen children, and seen most all sold off to slavery, and when I cried out with my mother's grief, none but Jesus heard me! And ain't I a woman?'

   (iii) 'Obliged to you for hearing me, and now old Sojourner ain't got nothing more to say.'

3. What effect on the audience is achieved by (i) repetitions, (ii) questions and (iii) exclamations? Explain your response.

4. Sojourner Truth speaks using colloquial (informal) expressions typical of her social class and background. Identify three examples of colloquial phrases used in her speech.

6. How, in your opinion, does the style of language used by Sojourner Truth add or take from the effectiveness of her arguments?

7. This speech lends itself to the use of various gestures, facial expressions, pace and tone of voice. Rewrite the speech, indicating clearly how you think a speaker should deliver it as part of a multi-media presentation on women's rights. Indicate any other elements of multi-media that could be used in such a presentation.

Speech 2

This extract is from a graduation speech former Apple CEO Steve Jobs gave at Stanford University in 2005. The extract highlights Jobs' considerable strengths as a speaker, a storyteller and inspirational leader.

I was lucky — I found what I loved to do early in life. Woz and I started Apple in my parents' garage when I was 20. We worked hard, and in 10 years Apple had grown from just the two of us in a garage into a $2 billion company with over 4,000 employees. We had just released our finest creation — the Macintosh — a year earlier, and I had just turned 30. And then I got fired. How can you get fired from a company you started? Well, as Apple grew we hired someone who I thought was very talented to run the company with me, and for the first year or so things went well. But then our visions of the future began to diverge and eventually we had a falling out. When we did, our Board of Directors sided with him. So at 30 I was out. And very publicly out. What had been the focus of my entire adult life was gone, and it was devastating.

I really didn't know what to do for a few months.

I felt that I had let the previous generation of entrepreneurs down – that I had dropped the baton as it was being passed to me. I met with David Packard and Bob Noyce and tried to apologise for screwing up so badly. I was a very public failure, and I even thought about running away from the valley. But something slowly began to dawn on me – I still loved what I did. The turn of events at Apple had not changed that one bit. I had been rejected, but I was still in love. And so I decided to start over.

I didn't see it then, but it turned out that getting fired from Apple was the best thing that could have ever happened to me. The heaviness of being successful was replaced by the lightness of being a beginner again, less sure about everything. It freed me to enter one of the most creative periods of my life.

Questions

1. What aspects of the extract suggest that it is perfectly suited for oral delivery to the intended audience of students at a graduation? Explain your response.
2. Complete the following statements about the above speech by choosing the most appropriate word from the options given. Give reasons for your choice.
   (i) Steve Jobs' style of speaking is (a) complex (b) accessible (c) obscure.
   (ii) The sentences in the extract are predominantly (a) compound (b) simple (c) complex.
   (iii) Jobs uses personal anecdotes to (a) amuse (b) inform (c) persuade his audience.

Unit 4: Literacy

3. In what way is the impact of the rhetorical question used in this extract similar or different to that of the rhetorical questions used by Sojourner Truth in Speech Extract 1? Explain your answer as fully as you can, placing focus on the purpose served by the rhetorical question/s.

4. Insert pauses at the points in the speech where you believe they would have the strongest impact on the audience.

5. What gestures, facial expressions and variation of tone of voice could assist in making the first paragraph more effective in its impact on the audience? Insert your suggestions as bracketed directions in the first paragraph.

Tip:
The full graduation speech is available on YouTube. Once you have answered the questions you may wish to view the speech and consider your answers again.

C. Visual Literacy

1. What is Visual Literacy?

Images 'speak' to us in a way that words do not. Most days of your life you are probably bombarded with images - pictures of you and your friends on social media; illustrations in magazines and books; posters, flyers, advertisements etc. You cannot actually escape them!

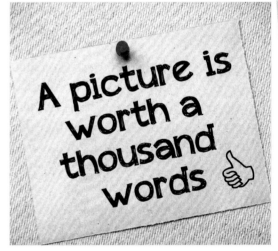

Visual literacy refers to your ability to interpret, question, challenge and evaluate texts that communicate with visual images alone or with an accompanying text.

Students who are visually literate can read the **intended meaning** in a visual text, **interpret** the **purpose** and intended meaning, and **comment on** the form, structure and features of the image.

In your final exam you may be asked to demonstrate your visual literacy skills by doing various types of tasks. You may be asked to:

● Write a detailed, **objective description** of an image or group of images.
● **Interpret** and respond **imaginatively** to an image.
● Use an image as a **stimulus** for a creative writing task such as a poem or the opening of a descriptive or personal essay.
● Use an image as a **setting** for the opening of a story.
● **Link an image or group of images to a written text,** showing how they relate to or illuminate each other.
● Comment on the **effectiveness of a poster or an illustration** for an advertisement.
● Relate an image to a **theme** and comment on its effectiveness.
● Select your **favourite** image from a selection of images (such as posters for a film), explaining your choice.

2. Analysing an Image

You will have developed your visual literacy skills during your Junior Cycle programme. The following material will help with your revision and exam preparation.

When presented with an image or group of images in the examination ask yourself questions such as:

- **What** or **who** is the subject of the image?
- **Why** am I being shown this subject?
- **What** am I being asked to do with this image?

In order to respond effectively, you will need a clear understanding of **visual language**:

Subject: The subject or dominant image is the central focus in an image. It is often, but not always, at the centre.

Shot: A shot refers to an image captured by a camera.

- A wide shot (sometimes, long shot) shows a more distant picture of a scene or subject. It can be used to portray the scale of a setting or to place a subject in a wide context
- A medium shot focuses the viewer more closely on the scene or subject by moving the camera position or by using a zoom lens.
- A close-up shot focuses on details of the subject or scene. This can help the viewer to interpret atmosphere or notice emotion in a subject.
- A cut-away shot moves from the subject to an observer or observers.

Angle: The angle of a shot refers to the position from which a camera views a subject. To get a high angle, the camera is directed down at the subject, making the subject seem smaller. In order to get a low angle, the camera looks up at the subject, which then appears to be larger.

Border: A border or frame is used to enclose a photograph or image. The border guides the viewer's eye towards the subject.

Depth: Images may appear to be two-dimensional or three-dimensional. Two-dimensional images look flat, whereas three-dimensional images have depth.

Describing an image

A picture description is an ideal way of practising your English skills and vocabulary. Remember you are writing **a factual description**, so do not engage in **interpretation**.

Guidelines for describing a picture:

- Have a close look at the picture and decide on how to structure your picture description. **What is the focus of the picture?** – what is important or special? What should the viewer pay attention to?
- Give a **general introduction** – *'This picture shows that ...' 'In this picture I can see ...'*
- Describe the **place or setting** of the picture e.g. *'I can see a rough path with a wooded area in the distance ...'*

- Use **adjectives** and comment on **colour**, **light and shade**, **atmosphere created**.
- Mention **the angle** from which a picture is captured - e.g. an aerial shot, a close-up etc.
- When describing **people**, mention their approximate age, clothing, gender, posture, actions etc.
- If people have **clearly defined roles**, state what these are. e.g. a teacher with a class of children, a doctor examining young, malnourished children, etc.
- Make sure that your picture description is **logically structured**, for example: from left to right (or from right to left) from the background to the foreground (or from the foreground to the background) from the middle to the sides (or from the sides to the middle).

Sample Question and Answer on a Description

Write a description of the image below

The picture depicts a small church, surrounded by trees and shrubbery. In the foreground of the picture, there is a still lake, which reflects the image of the small church. Fine ripples can be observed on the surface of the lake. The water is lighter to the right of the picture, where we see the reflection, and darker to the left. Small shrubs grow along the perimeter of the lake and the land.

The church can be seen in the middle ground, right of the picture. We see it from a side angle. It has a high-pitched roof, which appears to be made out of slate. The brick-work is grey and we can see a lighter brick, where the angles of the walls meet. One entry, facing slightly towards the left front, has been blocked up. The curved arc above this previous doorway and the sides can be clearly seen. The rest of this wall is covered in shrubbery. The church has double wooden doors, with a rounded arch entrance. Large bolted hinges can be seen, holding the doors in place.

There is a neat, well-kept lawn in front of the church. Small trees stand on the lawn and there is a small bench, supported by three legs or blocks. The background shows a low mountain, with channels created by little rivulets. The terrain is rough and wild and shown with a soft focus, which makes it appear blurred. There aren't any people in this picture. The atmosphere is one of serenity, beauty and calm

Write a detailed, objective description of each of the following images:

1.

2.

3. Writing a Dialogue based on an Image

You may be required to write a short dialogue based on an image. This should be written as a script.

Guidelines for writing a script based on an image:

- Give **names** or some form of identity to the people, animals or objects which are supposedly having the dialogue.
- Arrange the script by putting the name of each speaker in the **left hand margin** and writing a colon (:) after each speaker's name.
- Keep the characters' lines of dialogue short. Do not write large chunks of dialogue.
- **Conversational tone** is appropriate and you may use contractions e.g. *'I'm' instead of 'I am'*.
- Create as much **interest** as you can in the conversation, making each comment meaningful and moving the dialogue forward.
- **Do not insert unnecessary comments** e.g. 'Good Morning. How are you?', 'I'm fine. How are you?' etc. This makes for a very boring script. Be creative and original.

Sample Dialogue based on an Image

Write a dialogue based on the image.

[Characters are JENNY and CATHERINE. They are both young business women working for a large corporation.]

JENNY: It really isn't my imagination Catherine, they are excluding me and I don't know why.

CATHERINE: Listen, Jen, when I came here last year, I was convinced of the same thing. They aren't deliberately brushing you off. They have been here a few years now and have formed a close business relationship. They often discuss things together like that.

JENNY: Well I don't think it's very good manners to sit in a group, having conversations about things which I haven't the foggiest notion about. So much for team work! I feel like a spare part around here. How did you deal with it? You seem fine with them now.

CATHERINE: I felt a bit like you but I decided to pretend I didn't notice that they were ... well, sort of ignoring me. I inserted myself into their conversations, asked questions, made them tell me what was happening. I even offered opinions!

JENNY: I wish I had your confidence to make them take notice of my presence.

CATHERINE: If you like, I could have a word with them and let them know you feel a bit neglected.

JENNY: Catherine! That's very decent of you, but I wouldn't be comfortable with that. I think I'll just have to assert myself a bit more. Make them notice me.

CATHERINE: Well, if that's how you want it – but don't miss coffee break with us anyway. You're a bit shy you know.

JENNY: Thanks for the moral support Cath. I'm glad you're around here or I think I'd go crazy.

Write a short dialogue based on the following image:

4. Creating a Setting based on an Image

Sample Question and Answer based on an Image

Imagine that the picture below shows a setting for a story that you are writing. This setting is not as perfect as it appears to be. Write a descriptive passage for the opening of your story.

Although the sand was blistering hot under my feet, I still felt the chill of fear and isolation. The gentle sound of breaking waves mingled with the slight rustle of long grasses on the dunes. What secrets were they whispering? What tales were they telling? This place, which was once my idea of Paradise, had turned into a kind of hell. The pure blue sky above me, the golden sand beneath me and the sea birds calling in the distance gave me pleasure no more. The calm was now deceptive. It was cruel. It masked what had happened here and I had no choice now but to become part of the deception and hide in this beautiful place my ugly secret.

Tasks

The pictures below show the settings for two different stories. Choose one of the pictures and write a descriptive paragraph in which you create a picture of the place and give the reader a sense of the mood or atmosphere of that place.

1.

2.

5. Images in Advertising

Advertisements do not always use words to sell their products. Sometimes the illustration cleverly contains the appeal, creates the need and sells the product or service. You need to examine the visual for all its connotations if this is the case.

Guidelines for analysing an advertisement:

● First, ask yourself:

What is being advertised? A product or a service?

Who is it aimed at (the target audience)? Who is likely to buy the product?

What are the benefits for the buyer, according to the ad?

Where might this advertisement appear?

- Look at the **language used** in the text. What is the headline or main statement? Is there an effort to appeal to a person's self-image or emotions?
- Can you identify any use of flattery? Exaggeration? Rhetorical questions? Sensual appeal?
- Identify any repetition, key or buzz words, e.g. new, best, special, exclusive, bargain, etc.
- Is there **a slogan**? Where is it used and why?
- Is **humour used** in the advertisement? If so, how does this create an impact?
- Is there any stereotyping in the language or the illustration? How are the images connected to the text?
- Look at the **colours used** in the advertisement. Do these colours have any special connotations (associations) or effects on the reader?
- Look at any **people** in the advertisement. Are they happy, sad, lively, healthy, young, old, etc.?
- Have any 'experts' or celebrities been quoted or shown in the illustration?
- Examine body language, facial expression, clothing etc. Does the clothing suggest a particular image, e.g. a sharp suit = a business person; stylish clothes = a person interested in image and appearance?
- Is there a **logo**? Where is that placed and why?

Target market.

Tip:

AIDA is an acronym. It is a useful way to think of how to create a good advertisement.

A – Attention: Grab the attention of the customer.

I – Interest: Arouse customer interest by focusing on and demonstrating advantages and benefits of the product or service for sale.

D – Desire: Persuade customers that they need and desire the product or service.

A – Action: Stimulate customers towards taking action and/or purchasing the product or service.

Analysis of a Dove advertisement.

A The **attention** of the target audience is captured by the use of 12 colour photographs of the heads of women forming a box around the headline. The fact that the women are from different cultural groups, have different hairstyles and textures, have different coloured hair, wear their hair at different lengths and are different ages widens the appeal of the advertisement and creates variety.

None of these women are hair models. After all, neither are you.

Dove believes all women have beautiful hair when it's deeply cared for. No matter what length, style, cut, color or texture, you can discover the beauty in your own hair with the deep care in Dove Shampoos and Conditioners.
Learn more at www.campaignforrealbeauty.com

It is interesting to notice that only one woman could really be described as elderly, which suggests that the advertiser is placing more emphasis on youth and beauty in order to sell the product. Attention is also stimulated by the text placed within the photographic arrangement. The reader is directly addressed as 'You' which personalises the message and creates a friendly atmosphere.

I The **interest** of the customer is provoked by the use of words and phrases which have positive connotations – 'beautiful hair', 'deeply cared for', 'beauty in your own hair', 'deep care'. There is no doubt that the advertisement is suggesting that the product will provide exceptional care resulting in beautiful hair.

D The **desire** to use the product is created by the persuasive tone of the language and also by the fact that all the women in the pictures are smiling happily, which suggests that happiness is linked to having beautiful hair. The statement that women 'can discover' the beauty in their hair by using the shampoo suggests that they have not yet discovered that beauty and need to buy the product in order to do so. The emphasis on 'deep care' also suggests that the care provided by other products is not as good.

A **Action** is stimulated by encouraging the customers to 'Learn more' by visiting the website. The image of the product is carefully positioned in the bottom right-hand corner, (which is where the eye naturally rests when reading from left to right). One can clearly see what the container looks like, so it can be easily spotted on shelves in pharmacies or supermarkets.

Tasks

1. How is the text in this ad linked to the illustration?
2. Comment on the use of setting, colour and camera focus in the illustration.
3. Who is the target audience for this ad?
4. Where would you expect to find this ad? Give a reason for your answer.

6. Posters

A poster is any piece of printed paper, bill or placard usually displayed in a public place. The most important difference between the poster and other print advertisements is that the poster is aimed at the audience 'on the move'. A passerby will not stand to read the poster very carefully. The poster, therefore, must capture the attention and get the message across instantly. Keep in mind all the skills which apply to effective advertisements.

Posters can be used for purposes other than simply advertising. They can be used to raise awareness of important health or social issues, e.g., anti-smoking or anti-bullying campaigns, road-safety reminders, election campaigns, etc. The AIDA technique also applies to posters.

Features of a good poster:

- It grabs attention immediately.
- The message is communicated quickly and is not complicated.
- It convinces the reader of the benefits of the product/service.
- Colour is used effectively to hold the reader's attention.
- The KISS technique is used: Keep It Short and Simple.

Consider the general impact of the poster.

- Who would you say is the target audience for the poster?
- What does the poster want to achieve?
- Is the intention clearly communicated by the poster?
- Is the message of the poster communicated primarily by images or words?
- Is a political or social purpose served by the poster?
- What is your general opinion of the effectiveness of the poster?

Look at the following posters and answer the questions:

1. How does this poster grab the viewer's attention? Explain your response.
2. What is the message of this poster? Is it clearly presented?
3. Is this an effective poster? Explain your answer.

Source: Dublin City Council

7. Film Posters

Film Posters are more like advertisements and have a clear commercial purpose – to promote and encourage audiences to see a new film. When analysing a poster it is important that you judge both how well it achieves its purpose and how visually appealing it is.

Tips for analyzing a poster:

Step 1. Look closely at the poster.
- Get the big picture first before focusing on details.
- Examine the dominant colours used in the poster. What do they connote / suggest?
- Examine the main subject/figures/objects/background of the poster. Do they suggest an imagined or a real world?
- Check whether the messages in the poster are mainly visual, verbal, or both.
- Decide who you think is the targeted audience for the poster.

Step 2. Analyse the persuasive techniques.
- Decide which genre or type of film it is – horror, science-fiction, fantasy, comedy etc.
- What delights / thrills /gratifications are suggested by the poster?
- How does the poster grab your attention – humour, shock, surprise, famous actor/actress?
- If there is a tagline (slogan), how does the tagline work – humour, shock, pun, alliteration, etc.?
- Are there any quotations from reviews?

Step 3. Judge the quality of the poster.
- Does it communicate and appeal to you visually?
- Does it make you want to see the film?

Tasks

T

1. Read this short background to the film, 'Jurassic Park: Fallen Kingdom'.

   Three years after the destruction of the Jurassic World theme park, Owen Grady and Claire Dearing return to the island of Isla Nublar to save the remaining dinosaurs from a volcano that's about to erupt. They soon encounter terrifying new breeds of gigantic dinosaurs, while uncovering a conspiracy that threatens the entire planet.

2. Using the three steps outlined above, write a critical analysis of the poster for Jurassic World.

05 The Mechanics of Language

Introduction

Language is organized in different ways in order to create meaning. In your Final Assessment Examination, you will need to to apply your knowledge of language structures, for example, how to create well formed sentences and how to paragraph properly. You will need to show how you can use language appropriately, especially punctuation and spelling. You will need to demonstrate an understanding of how word order, grammar, text structure and word choice may change depending on the purpose of the piece of writing. This unit will help you to develop the skills you need to understand how language works.

A. Understanding Phrases and Clauses

1. Subjects and verbs

When we refer to a **subject** and a **verb** in a group of words, we are referring to the 'doer' (subject) of an action or state of being (verb).

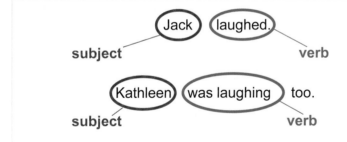

Sometimes the subject is implied rather than written.
                    Be quiet!
Here, the subject 'You' is implied: (You) Be quiet!

The part of the group of words containing the verb and telling more about the subject is called the predicate.

Tasks

1. Identify the subjects and verbs in the following sentences :
   (a) The family went to the cinema.   (d) Cathal scored the final goal.
   (b) Goldfish are inexpensive pets.   (e) Stay away from the water's edge.
   (c) Aisling enjoys playing tennis.
2. Write out sentences (a) – (e) underlining the predicate.

2. Clauses

A **phrase** is a group of words that <u>does not</u> have a subject and verb.
Example: fluffy baby chicks
A **clause** <u>does</u> have a subject and verb. **Example: Baby chicks are cute.**

There are two types of clauses:

1. An **independent clause** is a group of words that <u>can stand alone</u> and make complete sense.
   Example: The postman delivered the parcel.
2. A **dependent clause** <u>can't stand alone</u> and make complete sense. It depends on another clause.
   Example: When the postman delivered the parcel

A **sentence** uses clauses in different combinations which make complete sense.

- One independent clause (simple sentence):
  The boy played with his friends.
- Two clauses joined together with a conjunction (compound sentence):
  The boy played with his friends and went home for his dinner.
- A combination of independent and dependent clauses (complex sentence):
  When the boy had finished playing football, he went home for his dinner.

> Tip:
> Complex sentences always need commas or other punctuation marks to show different clauses. Phrases don't have a verb.

Tasks

1. Identify the phrases, dependent clauses and independent clauses in the following list (Note: all full stops have been left out):
   Example: I am staying at home this weekend = independent clause
   (a) When the party is over =
   (b) Before the match =
   (c) If there are too many people trying to get into the concert =
   (d) Stay away from the beach during the storm =
   (e) After my Leaving Cert =
   (f) Please try to hand your work in on time =
   (g) Although Martin is my cousin =
   (h) Because she arrived late so many times =
   (i) Learning to write well requires time and effort =
   (j) As the water burst from the broken pipe =
   (k) Most of the class are willing to take part in the fundraiser =

2. Identify whether each of the following are dependent clauses or independent clauses. (Note: all full stops have been left out):
   (a) If you want to communicate clearly =

(b) I hate walking to school in the rain =

(c) My friends and I are setting up a WhatsApp group =

(d) Because her mother asked Aisling to tidy up her room =

(e) The car needs to be serviced before the holidays =

(f) Don't create problems where none really exist =

(g) When the Leaving Cert results are known =

(h) If I won the lottery =

(i) The scene of the crash was horrific =

(j) Whenever we try to arrange a meeting =

B. Understanding Parts of Speech

In order to write well formed sentences, you need to understand the main parts of speech and the function they have in your writing.

1. Nouns, pronouns, adjectives, verbs and adverbs

1. A **noun** is used to refer to a person, place, thing, event, substance or quality.
Examples: Peter, elephant, chair, freedom, love, hope, etc.

2. A **pronoun** is used in the place of a noun or noun phrase.
Examples: I, you, he, she, it, we, you, they, them, those, etc.

3. An **adjective** is used to describe a noun or pronoun.
Examples: big, brave, evil, beautiful, sharp, etc.

4. A **verb** is used to describe an action or a state of being.
Examples: kicked, was, is, throws, swims, were, etc.
Verbs can be made up of more than one word: was eating, is going, had gone, will be coming, etc.

5. An **adverb** describes or gives more information about a verb, adjective, phrase or another adverb.
Examples: Adverbs of *manner*: quickly, slowly, wisely, truly, etc.
Adverbs of *place*: here, there, everywhere, somewhere, nowhere, etc.
Adverbs of *time*: soon, still, already, etc.

Tasks

1. Identify the parts of speech for each of the following words:

   (a) The fisherman caught some fine fish.

   fisherman _____

   caught _____

   fine _____

   fish _____

   (b) Michael trusted John because he knew that he was loyal.

   Michael _____

   trusted _____

   John _____

   he _____

   knew _____

   was _____

   loyal _____

2. Copy the table below into your copybook and place each of the following words in the correct column:

   China, was, basket, were, you, slowly, clever, quickly, wanted, year, wicked, somewhere, garden, played, she, John, it, shabby, summer, here, proud, told, soon, charitable, weeds, they, he, herd, Paris, still, comes, I, already, explained, hopefully, is, we, tried, wise, their, greedy, extremely, there, unkempt, foolish.

Noun	Pronoun	Adjective	Verb	Adverb

2. Prepositions, interjections and conjunctions

1. **A preposition is used to specify a location or a specific location in time.**

Examples:

above, below, throughout, outside, near, since, before, under, during, etc.

- The cat ran **under** the bed.
  The preposition 'under' tells us **where** the cat is.
- **During** the match, the supporters cheered their teams.
  The preposition 'during' tells us exactly **when** the supporters cheered.

2. An **interjection** is used to show a short sudden sudden expression of emotion.
Example:
Ah! Dear me! Wow! Oops! Hooray! Hey!

3. A **conjunction** (connecting word) joins or coordinates words, phrases and sentences.
When a conjunction joins words it always joins similar parts of speech e.g. nouns to nouns, adjectives to adjectives etc.
Example:
- This cake is <u>delicious</u> **and** <u>sweet</u>. The conjunction 'and' is joining adjectives.
- I don't know whether I left my keys <u>in my coat</u> **or** <u>in my car</u>. The conjunction 'or' is joining phrases.
- The boy was <u>poor</u> **but** <u>honest</u>. The conjunction 'but' is joining adjectives.
- I would like a house <u>on a hill</u> **or** <u>by a beach</u>. The conjunction 'or' is joining phrases.

A **coordinating conjunction** is also used for **joining two separate sentences.**
Example:
- I wanted to be her friend. She continued to ignore me.
- I wanted to be her friend, **<u>but</u>** she continued to ignore me.

When joining two separate sentences using a conjunction, **put a comma after the first sentence** and **do <u>not</u> use a capital letter** for the start of the second. Remember, you are making one sentence out of two.
Example:
- Tim had spent all his money. He had to borrow his bus fare home.
- Tim had spent all his money, **so** he had to borrow his bus fare home.

When using 'and' as a conjunction for short sentences, it is acceptable to leave out the comma.
The man was wearing a peaked hat **and** looked like a college student.

Tip:
To help you remember the most commonly used conjunctions you can use the word FANBOYS
F = for
A = and
N = not
B = but
O = or
Y = yet
S = so

Tasks

1. Join the following sentences using different conjunctions and making any necessary changes in word order:
   (a) I really want to go to school. I'm feeling too sick today.
   (b) There wasn't any milk in the fridge. There was nothing else to eat or drink.
   (c) Goldfish make good pets. They require very little maintenance.
   (d) He was becoming obese. He had to give up junk food altogether.
   (e) I didn't want to go out in the rain. My friends were expecting me to arrive for the party.

2. Learn the following poem to help you to remember parts of speech.

Every name is called a noun as 'field' and 'fountain', 'street' and 'town'.

In place of a noun the pronoun stands as 'he' and 'she' clap their hands.

The adjective describes a thing, as 'magic' wand or 'bridal' ring.

The verb means action, something done, to 'read' and 'write' to 'jump' and 'run'.

How things are done the adverbs tells us as 'quickly', 'slowly', 'badly' or 'well'.

Prepositions show relation as 'in' the street or 'at' the station.

Conjunctions join in many ways, sentences, words or phrase and phrase.

The interjection cries out 'hark!' I need an exclamation mark!

C. Understanding Punctuation

Correct punctuation is essential for writing to make clear sense. Compare how difficult it is to understand the first speech bubble (without punctuation) with the second speech bubble (with punctuation).

the fact is that no species has ever had such wholesale control over everything on earth living or dead as we now have that lays upon us whether we like it or not an awesome responsibility in our hands now lies not only our own future but that of all other living creatures with whom we share the earth

David Attenborough – *Life on Earth*

The fact is that no species has ever had such wholesale control over everything on earth, living or dead, as we now have. That lays upon us, whether we like it or not, an awesome responsibility. In our hands now lies not only our own future, but that of all other living creatures with whom we share the earth.

David Attenborough – *Life on Earth*

1. Capital letters A, B, C

1. Capital letters are used at the **beginning of a sentence.**
Examples:
- I am going to Germany next year.
- When we arrived at the station, we found that the train was crowded with passengers.
- They asked him if he was going to plead guilty, but he refused to answer.

2. Capital letters are also used for **proper nouns.** Proper nouns include personal names, titles, nationalities and languages, days of the week and months of the year, public holidays as well as geographical places.
Examples:
- Marita and I plan to visit Rome next Easter.
- I have never been to Italy before.
- Can you speak Irish fluently?
- The next choir practice will take place on Wednesday.

3. Capital letters are used for the **titles** of books, magazines and newspapers, plays and music.
Examples:
- 'Wuthering Heights', by Emily Bronte, is a strange, compelling novel.
- The Irish Times published an excellent review of the new film 'The Maze Runner'.
- The orchestra will perform Beethoven's Sixth Symphony at their upcoming concert.

2. Full stops, question marks and exclamation marks . ? !

1. Full stops are used for **closing sentences**.
Ensure that a sentence makes full sense before you insert the full stop. Avoid separating sentences with commas when a full stop is required.
Examples:
- The weather was awful last Saturday.
- There seems to be no end to wind and rain this February.
- When John came into the room, Aoife jumped up to welcome him.

2. Full stops are also used for:
- **initials in personal names:** W. B. Yeats, J. Alfred Prufrock, P.J. Keating.
- **after abbreviations of titles:** Prof. Murphy.
  If the abbreviation consists of the first and last letters of a word, no full stop is needed:
  Mr (Mister), Dr (Doctor)
- **after other abbreviations:** etc. (etcetera), Sept. (September), Wed. (Wednesday).
- **in email addresses:** www.fullstop.com

3. Instead of a full stop, use **question marks** for questions.
Examples:
- Why are you crying?
- Where did I leave my wallet?

4. Instead of a full stop use **exclamation marks** for urgent commands or expressions of emotion:
Examples:
- Watch out! The tree is about to fall.
- Oh no! I forgot Dad's birthday.
- Listen! Can you hear that noise in the attic?

Tip:
Don't use a full stop after a question mark or exclamation mark.

Tasks

Write out the following sentences inserting the missing capital letters, full stops, exclamation and question marks. (Note: all necessary commas have been included).

1. we always get the afternoon off on wednesdays
2. jill peters was my best friend in primary school
3. if you had done more preparation for your exam, your grade would have been much higher
4. why did john refuse the invitation to mary's birthday party
5. go away i told you before that you are not to come to my front door
6. john b synge wrote 'the playboy of the western world', which we are studying this year
7. have you seen the film 'children of men' it is well worth watching
8. wow where did you get that beautiful dress it looks perfect on you
9. dr john f sullivan is a specialist in lung diseases he encouraged me to give up smoking
10. i will miss clare's birthday in july because i am going to france for the summer

3. Commas ,

Commas are used:

1.
After introductory words or phrases.
Example:
Whether you like it or not, you have to finish your school project.

2.
Before a coordinating conjunction (FANBOYS) to mark the
place where two sentences have been joined.
Example:
The weather forecast predicted rain today, yet there is not a cloud in sight.

3.
To section off parts of a sentence that are not essential to its meaning.
Example:
Tonight's choir practice, I am sorry to say, has been cancelled.

4.
To separate items in a list.
Example:
I like to eat apples, bananas, pears and apricots.

5.
When you interject or address somebody in the course of a sentence.
Example:
What do you think, Mr Adams, of the new school rules?

6.
To separate days, months and years.
Example:
I was born on February 4th, 2003.

7.
To signal that you are going to use a quotation.
Example:
Romeo refers to Juliet as a, 'bright angel'.

8.
To show that direct speech is following or has just occurred.
Example:
Mark's father shouted angrily, 'Where do you think you're going?'
However, when the direct speech is first, use a comma before
closing the quotation marks.
Example:
'I don't want to have to say this again,' the teacher told the class,
'you should know the rules by now'.

Tip:
Never use a comma to join two independent sentences.
Use a comma and a conjunction instead.

It is very wet today. The picnic has been cancelled.
~~It is very wet today, the picnic has been cancelled.~~
It is very wet today, so the picnic has been cancelled.

Tasks

Insert commas in the correct places in the following sentences:

1. It is important to write clear simple sentences.
2. Chloe is bringing the sandwiches fruit and desserts to the party.
3. It was too expensive to go abroad so we decided to stay in Ireland this summer.
4. To be honest I wish you would be a little tidier.
5. The storm which lasted several days did enormous damage.
6. Our next meeting will be on the 10th August 2019 so you have plenty of time to prepare for it.
7. 'I'm not coming with you' she said angrily.
8. When I forgot my lines in the play I felt very embarrassed.
9. He turned to me and said abruptly 'Where is Maria today? She's supposed to be here.'
10. How long has it been Mr Jones since you sat for your final exams?

4. Apostrophes ,

Apostrophes are used:

(a) to show **possession**

Michael's hat – the hat belongs to Michael.

(b) to show **contraction**

I'm You're We're

I'm, you're, we're – leaving out a letter or letters in a word.

(a) Apostrophe + 's' to show possession

1. When we show who owns something or has a close relationship with something, we use an apostrophe + 's' after the name or the noun.
Examples:
The woman's daughter. Mary's camera.

2. If a singular noun already ends in 's', just add the apostrophe after the 's'.
Examples:
Yeats' poem. Odysseus' journey.

3. When the noun is plural, we put the apostrophe after the 's'.
Examples:
The boys' school. (more than one boy)
The girls' dormitory (more than one girl).

4. If a noun has its own plural form (e.g. children, women) insert the apostrophe before the letter 's'.
Example:
Children's games. Men's clothing.

5. Sometimes you need apostrophes for plurals of letters.
Examples:
My a's look like u's.
If there was no apostrophe, it would confuse the reader - My as look like us!

6. Possessive pronouns (yours, hers, theirs, its etc.) do not need apostrophes to show possession. Do not confuse the possessive pronoun **its** with the contraction of 'it is' or 'it has'.

(b) Apostrophes to show contraction

We use contractions (I'm, we're) in everyday speech and informal writing. In order to show contraction, insert the apostrophe where a letter or letters have been left out:
Examples:
Don't (Do not – letter 'o' has been left out).
I'm a student. (I am – letter 'a' has been left out)
We're in the same class. (we are – letter 'a' has been left out)
You haven't got your books. (have not – letter 'o' has been left out)
It's raining. (It is – letter 'i' has been left out)

> **Tip:**
> Don't confuse simple plurals of nouns with possession or contraction.
> In 'it's' use an apostrophe only for contraction of 'it is' or 'it has'.
> Examples: It's my fault. It's been a lovely day.

Unit 5: The Mechanics of Language

Tasks

T

1. Indicate whether the use of apostrophes in each of the following sentences is correct ✔ or incorrect ✗:

   (a) Paul's collection of poems will be published this summer. ☐

   (b) It's difficult for me to understand poems that were written before my time. ☐

   (c) The correct use of apostrophe's is a mystery to me. ☐

   (d) The sun was magnificent; it's rays were sparkling on the waves. ☐

   (e) Five students' poems will be printed in the next newsletter. ☐

   Junior Cycle 2017 Final Examination

2. Insert apostrophes where needed in the following sentences:

   (a) The dogs bark was worse than its bite.

   (b) Conans new bike is his favourite possession.

   (c) The girls bedrooms were extremely untidy.

   (d) Its important that you learn how to use an apostrophe.

   (e) Didnt you hear the doorbell ringing?

   (f) Mr Jones cat has been missing all week.

   (g) Shes very upset to hear that her cousins sick.

   (h) The mens department is on the third floor.

   (i) Childrens toys are expensive unless you buy during the sales.

   (j) Marie said the bracelet Jeff found was hers, but no manufacturers mark was on it.

5. Colons and semi-colons : ;

(a) A colon is used:

1. To introduce lists.
Example:
There are three good reasons why you should exercise: improved energy, endurance and personal well-being.

2. To separate two parts of a sentence when the second leads on from or explains the first.
Example:
He got the sentence he deserved: six months in jail.

3. To indicate a sub-title.
Example:
For Using Windows: A Beginner's Guide.

4. To indicate that some other information will follow.
Example:
Her character has two main qualities: assertiveness and common sense.

> **Tip:**
> A colon means 'that is to say' or 'this is what I mean.'
> You must have an independent clause before the colon.

Tasks

Write out the following sentences using colons where appropriate:

(a) I have many interests drama, art and film studies.

(b) She was a world class athlete a skiing champion.

(c) Colm valued only one thing his All-Ireland medal.

(e) I'd like you to do the following tidy your room, feed the cat and prepare the vegetables for dinner.

(e) There are two things about my neighbour that I like his tidiness and his good humour.

(f) I'd advise you to read the new book by John Holmes, 'Dublin City A Personal View.

(g) One problem was noted on my report card lack of punctuality.

(h) The Christmas hamper contained lots of goodies an iced cake, biscuits, chocolates and plum pudding.

(i) Buying a house is not easy a nightmare in fact!

(b) **A semi-colon is used:**

1. To mark a break that is stronger than a comma but not as strong as a full stop. Both the words before the semicolon and the words after it must be complete sentences that could be separated with a full stop.

Example:
Michael has a history test tomorrow. He can't go out tonight.

The reason Michael cannot go out is **directly related** to the fact that he has a history test next day. Therefore we use a semi-colon.

Michael has a history test tomorrow; he can't go out tonight.

Alternatively, you could use a **conjunction**:

Michael has a history test tomorrow, **so** he can't go out tonight.

2. Here are some more examples of sentences using semi-colons:

Marie said she was not at the shopping centre; however, many people saw her there.
The snow was three feet deep; therefore, the roads were impassable.
Call back tomorrow; your parcel should be here by then.
I work part-time to pay my fees; I don't have much time for socialising.

Tip:
Never use a comma to join separate sentences.

Tasks

Rewrite the following using semi-colons to join the sentences. Remember that the semi-colon is appropriate when the two sentences are directly related to each other. Semi- colons are sometimes used instead of coordinating conjunctions (FANBOYS).

1. Many houses were destroyed in the recent floods. Proper protection systems were not put in place.

2. Some people use a word processor. Others prefer to write with a pen.

3. Most of the supermarkets are closed for the bank holiday. You can purchase basic groceries at the corner shop.

4. You must pay attention to time-management in exams. Marks will be lost if you don't finish the paper.

5. I could hardly believe that I had passed the exam. I had done very little work.

6. Aoife has decided to be a vegetarian. She chooses the vegetable option when eating out.

7. Many Irish companies suffered during the recession. A number of businesses had to close down.

8. My younger sister enjoys being part of the school musical. She enjoys dancing and singing.

6. Inverted commas ' ' " "

Inverted commas can be single – 'x' – or double – "x".
They are also known as quotation marks, speech marks, or quotes.

Inverted commas are mainly used in the following cases:

1. To mark the beginning and end of **direct speech** (i.e., a speaker's words written down exactly as they were spoken).
Example:
'That,' she said, 'is nonsense.'

There should be a comma, full stop, question mark, or exclamation mark at the end of a piece of speech. This is placed inside the closing inverted comma or commas.
Examples:
'Can I come in?' she asked.
'Wait!' he shouted.
'You're right,' he said.
'I didn't expect to lose.'

2. To mark off a word or phrase that's being discussed, or that's being directly quoted from somewhere else.
Her new single is called 'February 3rd'.
What does 'meander' mean?

7. Brackets and dashes ( ) –

Brackets or dashes can be used instead of commas to separate extra information from the main statement or sentence.

Example:
- The car was travelling at 60 kilometers (approximately 37 miles) per hour.
  In this example, the information in brackets is **unimportant** but may help some readers.

Example:
- It is possible – indeed very likely – that the house will need to be demolished.
  In this example, the information between the dashes is **important** and is being emphasised.

If you do not wish to break the flow of your sentence, a pair of commas creates less distraction.

Example:
- My elderly aunt, who is quite frail, has been admitted to hospital.

Tasks

1. Rewrite the following passage inserting any missing punctuation.

    i approached her with a sweet smile and politely asked her why I should leave the shop

    have I done something wrong, which I'm not aware of i asked innocently should i have asked assistance to reach for the scarf she glared at me as if I was something from an unknown species she took great care to slowly look me up and down from my dazzling head to the tips of my boots

    this shop is not for the likes of you i know your type i cannot turn my back but you'll be off out the door without paying

    oh no I thought, not another one of these bigots i kept my cool though

    i know i said, it must be terrible to have things stolen by dishonest people who don't know the difference between mine and yours you'll be glad to hear i have never stolen anything in my life not many people can say that not even many people from your generation can say that

    how dare you you little, thieving... ill call the guards if you don't leave at once get out

2. Rewrite the following short extract inserting any missing punctuation.

    a look of perplexity appeared on gabriel's face it was true that he wrote a literary column every wednesday in the daily express, for which he was paid fifteen shillings but that did not make him a west briton surely the books he received for review were almost more welcome than the paltry cheque he loved to feel the covers and turn over the pages of newly printed books nearly every day when his teaching in the college was ended he used to wander down the quays to the second-hand booksellers, to hickey's on bachelor's walk, to web's or massey's on aston's quay, or to o'clohissey's in the bystreet

D. Commonly Confused Words

1. Commonly confused words

Read the meaning and example of the word in the Word 1 column and then read the meaning and example of the word in the Word 2 column.

Word 1	Meaning and example	Word 2	Meaning and example
accept	to agree, to receive: I accept your offer.	except	not including: Everybody is going except John.
advice	suggestions about what to do (noun): Take my advice.	advise	to recommend a course of action (verb): I advise you to work hard.
affect	to change or make a difference to something: If it rains, it will affect the match.	effect	a result; to bring about a result (in this case, noun): Smoking has a bad effect on your health.
aisle	a passage between rows of seats: The bride walked up the aisle.	isle	an island: I like the poem 'The Lake Isle of Innisfree'.
all together	all in one place, all at once: The visitors arrived all together.	altogether	completely, in total: He bought three books altogether.
aloud	out loud: I read my essay aloud in class.	allowed	permitted: You are not allowed to go to the party.
altar	a sacred table in a church: They brought the gifts to the altar.	alter	to change: Please do not alter the seating arrangements.
bare	naked, to uncover: It is not a good idea to bare your skin to the rays of the sun without protection.	bear	1. (verb) to put up with: I cannot bear the pain. 2. (noun) an animal: The bear came out of the forest.
born	having started life: The baby was born yesterday.	borne	carried or endured (suffer patiently): The illness was borne courageously.
bough	a branch of a tree: When the bough breaks the cradle will fall.	bow	1. to bend the head (verb): People bow to the king. 2. a decorative ribbon (noun): The girl had her hair tied back with a bow.
brake	1. a pedal for stopping a vehicle (noun): He hit the brakes. 2. to stop a vehicle (verb): She had to brake hard to avoid an accident.	break	1. to separate into pieces (verb): Sticks and stones may break my bones. 2. a pause (noun): I need a break from school.
cereal	a breakfast food made from grains: I eat a bowl of cereal every morning.	serial	Story that happens in regular instalments: My mum hates missing any episode from her favourite serial on TV.
chord	a group of musical notes: Mike taught me a new chord on the guitar.	cord	a piece of string: The parcel was tied with cord.

Word 1	Meaning and example	Word 2	Meaning and example
coarse	rough, rude: The drunk man spoke in a coarse manner to the police.	course	1. a direction: Follow the course of the river. 2. a series of lessons: We are beginning a new course in maths.
council	a group of people who manage or advise: Amy is on the student council.	counsel	advice (noun), to advise (verb):I was given good counsel regarding my choice of subjects.
curb	to keep something under control: You need to curb the money spent on sweets.	kerb	the stone edge of a pavement: The little boy tripped over the kerb.
currant	a dried grape: I love eating a currant bun.	current	happening now; a flow of water, air or electricity: He swam with the current.
desert	1. a waterless, empty area (noun), 2. to abandon someone (verb): I'd hate to be deserted in a desert.	dessert	the sweet course of a meal: The meal finished with a delicious dessert.
draught	a flow of air: There is a cold draught from under that door.	draft	an unfinished version of a piece of writing: You need to draft your essay a few times.
dual	having two parts: There is a new dual carriageway in my area.	duel	a fight or contest between two people: The men fought a duel to the death.
ensure	to make certain that something will happen: Please ensure that the room is left tidy.	insure	to arrange compensation against a risk: John insured his life for a large sum of money. It is necessary to insure your house against flood damage.
exercise	physical activity (noun), to do physical activity (verb): Everybody needs to exercise to maintain good health.	exorcise	to drive out an evil spirit: Not many priests are called on to exorcise evil spirits.
loose	wobbly or unstable: I have a loose tooth.	lose	to be unable to find: Did you lose your wallet?
our	belonging to us: This is our house.	are	from the verb 'to be': We are good friends.
pedal	1. a foot-operated lever (noun): Her leg was too short to reach the pedal. 2. to move a bike or car (verb): I like to pedal through the autumn leaves on my bike.	peddle	to sell goods: Many goods can be peddled in garage sales.
pour	to flow or cause to flow (verb): Pour some milk into the cat's dish.	pore	1. to study something closely (verb): Darren had to pore over the details of his contract carefully. 2. a tiny opening (noun): The pores on my nose are blocked.

Word 1	Meaning and example	Word 2	Meaning and example
practice	1. repeated exercise of a skill (noun): Practice makes perfect. 2. Exercise of a profession: Dr. Murphy has a large dental practice.	practise	to do something regularly to gain skill (verb): I am going to practise playing the piano every day because my music exams are next week.
principal	most important, the head of a school: Mr. Jones was appointed as school principal.	principle	a rule or belief: It is important to follow your principles in life.
quiet	making little or no noise: Be quiet!	quite	absolutely: are you quite sure about that?
sight	the ability to see: I could hardly believe the sight of my own eyes!	site	a location: That is a good site to build your house.
stationary	not moving: The van was stationary outside the shop.	stationery	writing materials: I must buy more stationery because I have letters to write.
storey	a level of a building: The house is three storeys high.	story	a tale or account: Children love to hear a story.
threw	past tense of the verb 'to throw': he threw the stone at the pig.	through	a preposition meaning in one side and out the other: The sun shone through the window.

Tasks

Correct the mistakes in the following sentences:

1. The boy kicked a ball threw the bedroom window.
2. If you take my advise, you will practice your spelling every day.
3. We are not aloud to go out tonight.
4. Did you loose your wallet?
5. The traffic accident had a terrible affect on the children.
6. Everyone is invited to the party accept Kevin, who is not aloud to come.
7. Who through that stone?
8. We had a tasty desert after the main meal.
9. What can we do about that draft from the back porch?
10. The principle of our school is a man of principal.

2. **More commonly confused words**

1.

There, Their and **They're** are homophones (words that sound the same but have different meanings).

(a) There always refers to a place or an action.
Does anyone live **there**? There will be a day off tomorrow. Put it over there.

(b) Their shows belonging or possession.
They put **their** books in **their** lockers. Their house is in the city.
I think they spend their money wisely.

(c) They're is a contraction of the words 'they' and 'are'.
They're on their way to the party. I will tell you if **they're** coming. They're almost there now.

> **Tip:**
> Replace the word <u>there</u> with either 'here' or 'was it/is it/will it'.
> Replace the word <u>their</u> with 'our'.
> Replace the word <u>they're</u> with 'they are'.
> If the sentence still makes sense, you've got it right.

(a) I will see you **there**.   I will see you here. *(It makes sense so you've got it right!)*
There will be a day   Will it be a day off tomorrow? *(It makes sense so you've got*
off tomorrow.   *it right!)*

(b) Their marks are good.   Our marks are good. *(It makes sense so you've got it right!)*

(c) They're going away.   They are going away. *(It makes sense so you've got it right!)*

2.  and

(a) Your is a possessive adjective. It is used to describe something as belonging to you.
It is usually followed by a noun. For example:
Is this **your** bag?
Your party really was a great success.
Did your exams go well?

(b) You're is the contraction of two words 'you' and 'are'. It is often followed by a verb ending in 'ing'. For example:
You're looking very well today.
You're going to be glad that you did your revision for the test.
I will go if **you're** going too.

3. and

Its and it's are often incorrectly used.

(a) **Its** shows possession, e.g. The dog buried **its** bone in the garden.

(b) **It's** is a contraction of the words 'it is' or 'it has', e.g. **It's** all his fault.

Rewrite the following sentences correctly.

1. Tracy and her sister are not allowed to have there friends visit they're house on weekdays.

2. There my friends over their.

3. Your not supposed to put those books their.

4. Its not fair to the rest of the team if your allowed to skip football practice.

5. Their is great excitement in Alan's house; its his graduation day.

6. The cat got it's paws wet in the garden pond.

7. You're dog is burying a bone in they're garden.

8. Its a pity you and you're friends don't take part in sports.

9. When your supposed to be working, you're friends are not supposed to ring your mobile.

10. Their not going for a picnic because its raining heavily.

4. Where and Wear

(a) The word **where** is used when asking a question about a location.
   Where are you going?
   Where is the cash kept?
   Where did you stay when you went away?

(b) **Wear** has a couple of meanings.
   It can refer to an article of clothing that a person is 'wearing'.
   I wouldn't **wear** that to a dog-fight!
   What will you **wear** today?
   Wear something special today.

   Wear can also mean to make tired or exhausted.
   She would **wear** you out!
   The **wear** and tear of life can be seen in the old man's face.

5. **We're** and **Were**

(a) The word **we're** is a contraction of the two words 'we' and 'are'.

We are coming tomorrow. → **We're** coming tomorrow.

We are playing together. → **We're** playing together.

We are best friends. → **We're** best friends.

(b) **Were** refers to something that happened in the past.

Where **were** you going?

Were you lost?

We **were** on the beach when it started to rain.

6. **To** **Too** **Two**

(a) **To** can be used in the following ways:

(i) A **preposition**, in which case it always goes **before a noun**, e.g. I am going **to** school. She is on her way **to** the house.

(ii) An **infinitive**, in which case it always goes **before a verb**, e.g. I am going **to** work during the summer holidays. He thought he was going **to** have the day off.

(b) **Too** can be used in the following ways:

(i) Another word for 'also', e.g. Mark would like to come to the party **too**. Jane worked in the supermarket **too**.

(ii) Another word for 'excessively', e.g. I am **too** tired to go for a walk. This soup is **too** salty.

(c) **Two** is the number that follows one. It has no other meaning.

7. **Of** and **Off**

(a) The words **of** and **off** are commonly confused.

The word **of** has several uses, but it is usually a preposition which expresses the relationship between a part **of** something and the whole, e.g. The sleeve **of** his coat is torn. I put it in the back **of** the car.

It is often used to point out what something is made of or what it contains, e.g. I ate a bag **of** crisps. She loves her cup **of** tea.

Tip:
You will know that you should use **of** if the **f** sounds like a **v**.

(b) **Off** is frequently used as an adverb or a preposition.

As an adverb, it is used usually to describe a state of finishing something, e.g. Turn **off** the light.

As a preposition it is used to show the physical separation or distance from two positions: Take those things **off** the table. The shop is just **off** the main street.

> **Tip:**
> You will know that you should use **off** if the f sounds like an f.

8. Double negatives

You should avoid using two negatives in a sentence, e.g. I **never** do **nothing** right. This should be: I **never** do anything right.

We **aren't** going **nowhere**.
This should be: We are going **nowhere**. Or: We **aren't** going anywhere.

I **didn't** do **nothing**.
This should be: I **didn't** do anything. Or: I did **nothing**.

Check your sentences to make sure that you only use one negative.

9. Would Should Could

Would, should and **could** are auxiliary verbs. This means that they help or assist main verbs. For example, in the sentence, I would like an **ice-cream**, 'like' is the main verb assisted by **would**.

These three words are the past tenses of will (**would**), shall (**should**) and can (**could**). Be very careful to use the past tense correctly: **would** have ... should have ... **could** have. (Do not fall into the trap of using 'of' with these verbs instead of 'have'. It is never right to use 'of' with these verbs.)

Tasks

Rewrite each of these sentences correctly:

1. Wear is you're school uniform?

2. Too of the team could not attend the meeting because they where sick.

3. Take of your coat when you come into the house.

4. Do you we're warm clothes in the winter?

5. Its two late too apply for the summer job.

6. Your going to be very happy when you get the day of school.

7. I love a cup off tea with my too biscuits.

8. I forgot were I put my books.

9. Jack would like to go too the disco to.

10. My mother doesn't think those shoes will where well.

11. He should of put his books in his locker.

12. If I'd had a choice, I would of liked to learn music.

Sample Question and Answer

5 marks

1. In each of the following sentences, one of the homophones used is correct and one is incorrect. In each case circle the one homophone that is correct. Homophones are words that sound the same but have different meanings. The first example has been completed for you.

   (a) (Two) / too rabbits appeared out of the magician's hat.

   (b) The pupils placed there / their coats on hooks and sat down quietly.

   (c) I had to alter / altar my costume before the show.

   (d) My brother is so proud, he finally passed his test and got his driver's licence / license.

   (e) I stood at the end of the pier / peer and watched the sunset.

   Junior Cycle Final Examination 2018

   English – Higher Level